Lauren's Story

An American Dog in Paris

Kay Pfaltz

J. N. Townsend Publishing
Exeter, NH
2005

Originally published as a hardcover edition.

Cover photo by Ted Pfaltz.

Published by:

J. N. Townsend Publishing
4 Franklin Street
Exeter, NH 03833

800/333-9883

www.jntownsendpublishing.com

Distributed to the trade by Alan C. Hood & Co.
www.hoodbooks.com

ISBN: 1-880158-50-7

ACKNOWLEDGEMENTS

Special thanks to my mother, Susan Ordway Pfaltz, my father John Lucas Pfaltz, my brother Ted, and my sister Amy, and my publisher Jeremy Townsend.

Printed in Canada

For Amy

*Un souvenir heureux est
peut-être sur terre,
plus vrai que le bonheur*

—Alfred de Musset

PARIS

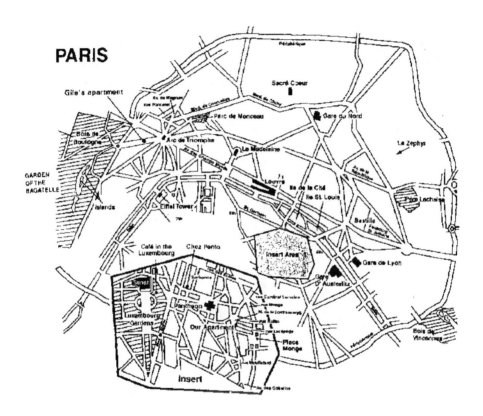

Périphérique

Sacré Coeur

Gile's apartment

Av. de Wagram
rue Poncelet
Bord. de Courcelles
Parc de Monceau
Bord. de Clichy

Gare du Nord

Bois de
Boulogne

Arc de Triomphe

Le Madeleine

Le Zephys

GARDEN
OF THE
BAGATELLE

Av. des Champs Elysée

Louvre

Av. de la
République

Islands

Eiffel Tower

Ile de la Cité
Ile St. Louis

Père Lachaise

7th

St. Germain

Bastille

Café in the
Luxembourg

Chez Pento

Insert Area

Gare de Lyon

Gare
D'Austerlitz

Sénat

Luxembourg
Gardens

Panthéon

Sorbonne

rue Cardinal Lemoine
rue Monge
M. de la Contrescarpe
rue Rollin

Our Apartment

rue Lacépède

Bois de
Vincennes

Place
Monge

rue Mouffetard

Insert

Av. des Gobelins

Prologue

In the hour of dawn the air is chill but pure. I look out to the awakening city, nineteenth-century buildings cast in gray light, as the waiter places a steaming *café crème* before me. I take the first hot sip of the mixed coffee and milk, and a Proustian flood of memory runs through me. It tastes like it always does. Like the first time.

Across the square, the owner of the *pâtisserie* dumps a bucket of soapy water upon the sidewalk. On the balcony above, an orange cat watches thoughtfully as if posing for a Doisneau photograph then turns its attention to some pigeons fluttering around the building's perky chimney pots. I take another sip.

A friend had asked me to write an article about the meaning of unconditional love. I set the cup down. I'd sat at this table before, many years ago. She'd sat in the basket-woven seat next to me. I can see her eyes, fixed with abiding hope upon the croissant as though it might leave the plate on which it lay. I guess Paris will always remind me of Lauren.

I always said that my happiest moments were spent with her beside me. Many of these were at restaurants. Once I attempted to count and name all the restaurants we'd dined in together—sometimes with my friends, but in most cases, just the two of us—dog and human together. I lost count after eighty-four. I know there were more I'd forgotten. I remember well the first time, and the birthday celebrations, the great restaurants: Taillevent and Robuchon, and the ones where I was a regular and they loved her. The most memorable? Every time was different, and yet very much and wonderfully the same:

"*C'est un vieux copain.*" The waiter did not ask, but rather stated, wistful, perhaps remembering his own dog.

"*Oui,*" I did not correct him. Many people assumed she was a male, I think because the breed beagle is a masculine one, just as a maltese seems feminine.

"*Vous avez choissi?*"

"*Oui, je prendrais la salade folle pour commencer, et ensuite l'andouillette.*"

"*Ah, l'andouillette, très bien.*"

I asked for water for Lauren, even though I knew she wouldn't drink till every scrap of food was removed. The waiter smiled at her and left.

She never lay down. She always sat upright, beside me on the banquette or in her own chair. She only fell off a few times. I would talk to her and she'd look into my eyes, never doubting a word I said, while the neighboring tables looked over with a fond curiosity mixed with respect. Parisians have an unparalleled preoccupation with their dogs. I guess in that way I came the closest to being a true Parisian. I always felt more Parisian than anything else, but I never was. There was the perverse comfort of not belonging anywhere. What was it Gertrude Stein had said? "America's my country, but Paris is my home town," or something like that. For what seemed to me like a long time, but in actuality when laid out against the time charts of history would be considered a brief period, Paris was to become home to Lauren and me.

The best conversations I had were with Lauren. Her searching and soulful eyes would get me thinking and talking about philosophy in a way I didn't with my friends. Did I love dining with her because I could talk about what I wanted and she always listened, perhaps even finding me entertaining? Do we love our animals because they do not complain to us, do not criticize us, and do accept us for who we are no matter what faults? Undoubtedly, yes. But with them we also experience the most *pure* relationships of which we humans are capable.

The church has debated for centuries the question of whether or not animals have souls. Of course in an animal lover's mind there is no question about it. Look at the animal you love. Every time I looked into Lauren's brown eyes I saw more soul than I do in most humans. The very word animal comes from *anima*, Latin for the soul. Enough said.

The food arrived and, crazy as she was about food, for when she was found she was nearly dead from starvation, she sat patiently beside me and awaited her own bites. The love and respect I felt for her grew throughout our lives together.

Many times the chef himself would walk out to see her. Once at La Coupole, the first restaurant in which Lauren ever dined, Jeanne

Moreau was celebrating her birthday, surrounded by film-star types. The chef came out, although it was not to Mme. Moreau he went first, but to Lauren. He called her *sage*. This was only one of many times I was to hear that word describe my dog. The word *sage* in French means far more than merely our "wise." It translates to well-behaved, virtuous, sensible, prudent, wise, good and, most of all, gentle. Lauren came to exemplify the full meaning of the word *sage*.

I tilt my cup and drink the last bit of liquid, now almost cold. I get up. Unconditional love. I'll give it a shot.

Chapter 1

The greatest gift I ever received was a strange, little dog. Her name was Lauren.

The first time I ever heard of Lauren I was in my apartment in Paris and my boyfriend of the minute had just broken up with me, for what seemed the eighty-eighth time. My sister Amy had been telling me to get a dog, get a dog. She said it would ease the loneliness, and I'd have something to care for, something to love, and something to force me out of the apartment. It would be a constant companion she said. Amy got a dog whenever she got depressed. That was her answer to life's curve balls. She had eleven dogs.

The phone rang and thinking it my boyfriend, or ex-boyfriend rather, I raced for it. It was Amy.

"You should get a dog," she said as I lifted the receiver. She must have had some extra sense to have known how bad things were.

"I don't want a dog. I want someone to *talk* to over candlelight dinners, someone to go to the movies with, someone—"

"Little Autumn and I talk," she interrupted.

"Interesting conversation, I want stimulating conversation, ideas—"

"Autumn and I have stimulating conversations all the time."

"That's you talking with yourself. You're starting to get eccentric, Amy."

"Don't be such a *fluss pferd*." She brought out the insult, which had now become an endearment, from our childhood. The *fluss pherd* or "river horse" was German for hippopotamus. When we were children we couldn't get over the fact that some German had thought the hippo was a horse who lived in the river, and called him, of all things, a *river* horse! We loved how the two words rolled off our tongues and had, for a spell, gone around calling anyone—adults, old ladies, you-name-

11

it—*fluss pferds* until one day our mother said, "Okay children that's enough," when one elderly lady from the neighborhood complained that we were evil, calling her dirty words, and we'd go straight to the devil. My mother suggested we go look up another word, "How about Rhinoceros. But you don't have to use it on our neighbors." I think we did look up Rhinoceros, but it mustn't have had the same ring as *fluss pferd* for I don't remember the word today.

"Amy, I'm not a *fluss pferd*. I just don't think a dog is what I'm looking for or the answer to my current problems. No offense to your coping mechanisms," I added.

"You never listen to me in the times you most need it. One day you'll see. Remember hindsight has…"

"…twenty-twenty vision," I finished for her.

"Well, *learn* from it. Don't keep making the same mistakes."

"You mean learn from you."

"Of course."

We hung up, but she phoned me back the following evening, excited.

"I have the dog for you! Her name's Lauren and she's adorable."

"Who's Lauren?"

"She's a little beagle, and you're gonna love her."

"Hold on a minute."

Beagles were a dime a dozen in Virginia where I had grown up and where Amy still lived. They were used as hunting dogs, and sometimes badly treated. Many were strays or came from beagle colonies where the dogs were used to test new products, some never seeing the outside light. Beagles were used in the colonies because they were small, friendly and even-tempered. Mostly they were tortured in the testing, injections shot into them, livers tied to their backs, minuscule cages, no windows. I didn't like to think about those beagles.

"She a colony escapee?"

"Probably!" Amy liked that.

"Really, where'd you find her?" I asked.

"She found me. Well Autumn found her, really." Little Autumn was my sister's little terrier who I called, much to Amy's horror, a little bag of rags. "I was late for work but Autumn kept barking at something under the porch, so I went to investigate. That's when I saw her. She was unconscious, nothing but bones, covered in fleas. I checked her gums, white as they could be, so I knew I had to move quickly. If I'd have found her thirty minutes later, she would have been dead."

I didn't realize then, as Amy spoke, the magnitude of this single statement. I didn't realize my destiny was being shaped. I only asked, "How'd she get the name Lauren? She have tags?"

"No, because of Bogie," Amy said, exasperated by me. "She's a little female, 'course she'd be Lauren."

Bogie was Amy's token beagle. Although she loved him now, she hadn't wanted him when he arrived. He too had turned up at her old, white farmhouse. I think there must have been a tacit knowledge among stray dogs that this was a house where they could come and be taken in and fed and eventually given a good home. Many turned up on her doorstep. But Amy loved sight-hounds. She didn't want a beagle, much less two. Bogie arrived with a shattered kneecap, and, after two operations and more than two thousand dollars, the vets informed her they could do no more and she would have to put him down. She agreed, so together she and Bogie drove off to end his life as a beagle. Bogie sat beside her in the front seat, stoical and brave, and that's how he got his name, after Humphrey Bogart. They never made it to the vets. Amy turned the car around, spent more money on operations, and Bogie grew up just as happy and healthy as her other dogs. But he never again lived up to his name.

Naturally Lauren was named after Lauren Bacall. She never lived up to her name either.

"Where's Lauren now?" I ventured, curiosity overtaking sense.

"She's in intensive care. They wouldn't touch her until I raced back and got Apache to do a blood transfusion." Apache was Amy's German shepherd and, although it would take me years, I did finally figure out why Lauren always loved or developed crushes on big, male German shepherds. I think it was the shepherd blood inside her. "Kay," my sister continued. "They wouldn't even give her a *bath* for fear she'd die right there in the tub. I mean, picture a tiny, flesh and bones dog, almost dead."

"A plenary flea fest in the making."

13

"Yeah, whatever. I drove so fast to get home—I really thought she'd be gone when I returned." And years later when I'd get Amy to tell me the story over and over, I'd involuntarily hold my breath, as if willing Lauren to live and become a part of my life. "She has some disease," Amy continued, "like AIDS, where her blood cells keep attacking her immune system." She paused. "The vets said she's probably not going to make it, but I thought she ought to have a home to go to, just in case."

"I don't need a dog."

"Well, I can't take her. Maybe I forgot to tell you, but I just got two new ones."

"Amy!"

"Hmmmm?"

"You said you weren't getting any more!"

"These are the last."

"You said that the last time."

"Circumstances alter cases."

"In other words you changed your mind."

"I have that right. And you're changing the subject. You need a dog. You need Lauren."

"Look Amy, for one thing I prefer *big* dogs, and besides I couldn't pop on a plane to another country when I felt like it if I had a dog."

"With a small dog you could!" Amy argued with me on that one, like she did with every objection I raised. Amy was categorical on her subject: the many benefits of dogs.

That's how it all began.

Lauren stayed in intensive care for three weeks. It was touch and go every day. Would her hermatocrits be up or down? Would she make it or not? Doctors John and Kathy, the husband and wife vet team fell in love with her, as would many in her years to come, and saved her life. They absorbed some of the costs, alleviating Amy of what would have been enormous fees she could not have paid. This practice was unheard of in the veterinary world, for if all stray, sick or injured dogs who were brought in were taken care of, the hospitals would go out of business.

But I had not thought much about Lauren after the phone conversation except to ask Amy once in a while when she called how the little beagle was doing.

As Lauren began to recover, my sister pressed me harder to take her.

"You'll love her."

But I didn't want a dog.

Then she sent me the photograph. I still have that photo. We call it the orange one, because Lauren sits on a scrap of orange cloth out in Amy's back yard. It was love at first sight. Never had I seen a more vulnerable looking animal. She was skinny and pathetic, yet the expression on her face and in her big eyes was one of acceptance. Acceptance is different from resignation. Lauren had suffered and she, like most animals, had accepted it. She'd had no choice. I wanted to pull her close to my breast, stroke her, and never let her go.

I noticed a shaved spot on her front leg where the I V had been. How could I have known then the significance of that mark? That she would, over the years to come, rarely be without that shaved rectangle on her front leg, or, as time went on, on three out of the four white legs.

I phoned Amy when I got the picture.

"I want her." I was serious. Now I was afraid that Amy would give her to someone else, for she'd been asking all her friends when I'd been reluctant.

Amy was excited. She felt vindicated.

"She's perfect for you."

"Yeah, I showed the picture to Jason and *he* even thought she was cute."

"Cute as lace pants."

"Lauren," I whispered, ignoring Amy, who I knew didn't like my current boyfriend, and looking at the photograph. The little dog in the picture was three colors: black, brown and white. Black and brown were the colors of its back and sides, leaving its underside all white. It was perched on tentative white legs and so thin I could count each vertebrae in the backbone. It had a crooked tail, with a white tipped end, big brown eyes that appeared to be lined with an eye pencil, and a beautiful brown face and head. But it was the look in the eyes that moved me the most. It looked lost.

This was the beginning of a love story.

And yet I would not end up with Lauren for more than a year.

Amy phoned back a few days later.

"So when are you going to take her?"

"Jason broke it off with me again today."

"All the more reason you need Lauren," Amy joked, but I knew she could hear the pain in my voice.

"I can't take her. I asked at work, and normally a dog would be fine—-it is France after all. But one woman brought her dog and it pooped all over the floor every day, so they had to set a policy. I'm too late, I'm afraid."

"Well, you could still take her," she urged.

"I wouldn't do that to her. She'd have to stay alone in this apartment all day long while I went to work."

"You ought to take her." Amy was becoming perturbed with what she thought my obstinacy, I could tell.

I felt so bad, I couldn't think about a dog. I wanted to talk with Jason, but knew I couldn't phone him. I couldn't bring myself to tell Amy how awful I really felt, but I knew she knew. We said goodbye.

Amy took in Lauren as one of her own, but always kept up the hope that I would one day take her. She didn't need another dog. As the months went by, however, Lauren became a part of the big dog family and Amy stopped trying to find her a home. She loved her. To give her away now would hurt.

Chapter 2

One year later, I walked across the Luxembourg gardens en route to the six *arrondissement* where I worked. I stopped and sat in a chair in front of one of the many works of art: a French garden. The Luxembourg was my haven. When life overwhelmed, I came here to find a bench or one of the green iron chairs and sit. Pathetic fallacy or not, the trees extended their boughs and offered me the understanding I sought and found lacking from the façades of stone buildings, however beautiful. In late-afternoon the light stretched out making funny shadows of the mothers pushing prams. The fountain splashed languidly into the *bassin* behind me, and the little wooden boats sailed around with great direction. The chestnuts stood majestically, protecting me as I gazed without thought at the palette of colors before my feet. *Fatina tarde.* The Italians had two words for this way of life and it could describe workers plastering walls or couples making love. Make haste slowly. People strolled to and fro before me. The Europeans *used* their parks and gardens; they were extensions of the living room.

A glance at my wrist told me I still had some time, so I took out *Le Monde* and started to read. I tried to absorb the news, but could not. The black print on the page turned red when I shifted my eyes. Even though the air was still cool, the sun was bright. But because of the latitude, the weak Northern European light was not as strong as what I was used to in Virginia. I learned to appreciate the tentative rays of sunlight. It was all the more gratifying and somehow poignant. I put my head back and closed my eyes and saw orange behind my eyelids. Then I heard the most beautiful sound I know of on this earth, the first three chirps of a bird at the start of spring. If life was this beautiful, then why was I not laughing out loud like the children I watched in the grass?

I leapt up and walked quickly to work.

Jason and I were once again back together, but he kept breaking up and I didn't know why, so I felt the transient quality of life, mine in particular.

I walked along the creaking wooden floor boards to my office, but once behind my desk I found I couldn't work. I glanced over to Jason's vacant desk, then let my hand reach for the phone.

"Hello?" When I heard his voice, I pressed the phone closer to my ear.

"Hey, it's me. Let's have dinner together."

"Kay, I, uh, I can't."

"Oh come on. I haven't seen you in a week. Are you all right?"

"I'm fine. But I've made other plans."

"Who could be more important than me?" I teased her, but felt my stomach tighten.

"Kay, there's something I've been meaning to tell you. Look, I didn't want to do it like this over the phone, but— But I can't see you anymore."

I said nothing and waited for him to continue.

"Kay, I really love you and all..."

"But?" I was confused.

"But there's a twist," he said quietly.

"What?"

"I'm married, Kay."

I tried to speak, but he spoke for me. I was glad.

"I made a mistake. I fell in love with you. I'm sorry if I've hurt you, but that's how it is. I can't see you anymore. I've made up my mind for good this time. Now you know why."

"I see."

"Don't try to see me. I can't."

"Jason, we work together."

"You'll have to resign. Please. You have to. The situation is unbearable. Do it for me."

"I like my job."

"But you like me more. Please, Kay."

"Jason—"

"I'm sorry," he said again and I could hear something crack in his voice. "Kay I have to go." Click. The phone went dead on the other end of the line. The receiver looked funny in my hands. I left my office quietly and went next door to the Rotonde where we'd always met. He'd never invited me home. Now I understood why. I remembered the last time we'd sat here side by side, sipping aperitifs. Sensing even then something was wrong, I'd been uneasy.

When I walked back home I had to circle around the Luxembourg gardens for it was just dusk and they had closed. It was the time *entre chien et loup* when it's no longer light, but not yet dark. Normally I loved this time of day, or night. Tonight I was lonely and sick at heart. Sitting in the café, I'd had two Kronebourgs, something I rarely did, drinking when depressed. But I found that it had helped. Tomorrow I'd think differently. I walked past *MacDoes*, French slang for MacDonalds, and up the rue Soufflot past the cafés where couples laughed and touched and kissed each other, then gazed into each other's eyes, and I wondered if anyone would ever gaze into mine like that. They came at me, coupled, holding hands, down the street. I walked by the illuminated Pantheon, standing alone just like me, and at that moment I knew I'd never belong anywhere. I'd never belong to anyone.

I walked into the empty apartment and sat down. Empty, always empty.

By the next morning all I felt was that I had to do something. I had to get out. I ran out and up the rue Blainville, back past the Pantheon. I passed its majestic neo-classical façade. Liberty, fraternity and equality for everyone, sure, I thought to myself. Your boyfriend tells you on the phone that actually he's married. It must have slipped his mind when the two of you met. Now you have to resign. I headed straight for my sanctuary, the Luxembourg gardens.

I walked by the statue of George Sand and whispered goodbye. Then past Baudelaire and the Statue of Liberty, and the bees in their beehives. I walked past the espaliered fruit trees, past the Medici fountain. I realized I was saying goodbye. I was leaving the Luxembourg gardens. Seven years of walking across during every season and every possible time of day. Goodbye to the chestnuts. Goodbye to the lindens. The situation was unbearable; he was right. And it had been for years,

I'd just been too blind to notice. I knew I was leaving my job for Jason. I loved him, or thought I did. I also knew I was being stupid, for I loved my job. But I was a romantic then and I am still today. It's what he wanted me to do; it's what he knew I would do. I regret nothing, however. I suppose that's what's important. My life would not have taken the course it did had I remained in Paris then. And there was someone else I was destined to meet.

Goodbye to the Orangerie. Goodbye Marie de' Medici, standing solid through all the turmoil. I'd lived in Paris long enough. I was going back to the States.

I called Amy that evening and told her what Jason had said.

"How dare he be married!" Amy was furious.

Amy dropped everything that was going on in her life to fly over to Paris and be with me as I packed. She knew what it would be like for me. She said very little while there, but the fact was, she was there.

She made me pickle sandwiches, a feat since Amy didn't cook, but they'd been my favorite as a child, and my sister assumed my tastes hadn't much matured.

I knew I was not a bad person, but I sure felt bad. How could I have been so stupid not to have seen the situation for what it was? I guess wishful thinking blinds us to blatant realities.

A line from *The Divine Comedy* kept going through my head:

> Hence thou mayst understand that love must be
> the seed of every virtue in you, and of every
> deed that deserves punishment.

Somewhat less poetical than Dante I said to Amy, "Love sucks."

"Gee Hon, that's descriptive."

"Love's hard."

"Original."

"Darn it! I don't want to think. I'm feeling too much right now."

"I see."

"I wasn't made for love. Something's wrong with me."

Amy rolled her eyes.

"I'll never find love."

"Relax Kay. You'll love again. Trust me."

I didn't.

One morning I went down to retrieve the mail and I found in an envelope the gold Cartier cufflinks I had given Jason. No note. Slowly I trudged back up the stairs and in through the door of my apartment. I sunk down onto the sofa and Amy sat down beside me. I wanted to leave, yet I didn't want to. How could I leave the city I loved so much?

"You'll get to look at trees again." Amy constantly tried to look on the bright side because I would not. She knew I loved the country.

"Paris has more trees than any other city except one," I replied. I'd forgotten what that other one was, and I kept wondering. Strange what you remember in times of stress.

"You'll get to see Lauren."

I didn't care about Lauren, I wanted Jason. But I said nothing, so not to hurt her feelings.

"It seems like bad stuff runs in waves," I said to Amy.

"Yeah, the first bad thing happens, and you're down so you attract more bad, vicious cycle, life's cyclical. When you're up, you attract good. Fast or famine."

"I think it's *Feast*—"

She shot me a look. "In your case fast seems appropriate." When she saw that I didn't appreciate this, she said quickly, "Tell me a joke." I loved telling jokes, but all my family made fun of my jokes, saying they were puerile.

"Okay," I began. "A man has a flink of cows—-"

"No! Not the flinking cow joke. There's no such thing as a flink. It's a herd."

"A flink is twelve or more cows."

"You made that up. It's a herd."

"Flink."

"Herd."

"Okay, I'll tell another." I thought for a moment. "Okay, ready?"

She shook her head. "Can't wait."

"Two peanuts were crossing Central Park—"

"No!" she shrieked. "No, Kay, not that joke, no, no, no. It's the worst joke I've ever heard."

I waited till her back was turned then whispered, "One was a salted."

She covered her ears in mock anguish.

"Okay, what's a cow with—" I started another, but was laughing so hard I couldn't get it out.

"I've never known anyone with a more immature sense of humor. Those are terrible! You're the only one who ever laughs at your horrible little jokes. I'm glad you're so easily amused. Guess if you went to prison or something…"

"Prison?"

She shook her head and raised her eyebrows, "Well, you never know…. Anyway, you could sit around telling yourself awful jokes and never be bored." But Amy had a hard time talking, for she too was laughing, and I thought of the great French actress Arletty's oft quoted words, "Loving one another means laughing together."

Chapter 3

When I arrived in Virginia I stayed at my mother's. An excellent and inventive cook, my mother made meals for me, talked to me, but didn't pry. The thirty-four acres in the country where she lived succored me. I watched the sunrise and sunset every morning and night that I could, for in Paris rarely could I see this that I loved, and I had missed it. I had also missed my family. My brother Ted lived only seven miles away. I got to spend time with him. He makes me laugh. He also makes me think more than anyone else I know. I had missed his witty company.

My father doesn't make me think because he's so smart he thinks for me. He can answer any question I ask him about history, science, philosophy, you name it. One day he'll win the Nobel Prize for something. I took after my father the most, except for the brains bit—there, the apple fell far from the tree.

Spending time with my family had been a luxury when I lived in Paris. Now it was an actuality that felt, in the way that only those feelings forgotten from disuse can, unexpectedly good. My sister was thrilled to have me back in the States. A few days after I'd returned, I went over to her house.

People always said they could tell we were sisters, but I could never figure it out. I thought I looked like neither Amy nor Ted. Amy was like something the Gods had accidentally dropped to earth. She had golden, sun-drenched hair, hazel eyes and every limb, finger and toe, was perfectly formed. She had an aura, like the sheen on an old walnut table that seems to exist apart from the table itself. But it wasn't so much this as it was the fact that she was completely oblivious to her appearance and, by extension, to her effect on the outside world of living, breathing, McDonald's eating, red-light running males. It seemed to me she lived a completely carefree life, beyond the constraints of society to which the rest of us were forced to adhere.

My sister's looks often misled people into believing she was brainless. She wasn't. At the age of seven, she'd read *The Odyssey* her only mistake being that she pronounced Penelope *Pen*-a-lope, the entire time in her mind, having never heard the name spoken aloud. Now if ever she gave me a hard time, all I had to say was "Shut up, *Pen*-a-lope." I stored it deep in my pocket, firing away when I really needed it.

"I want to show you something," she led the way. "Look."

"Oh, you got Little Autumn a new bed. Wow, her name's embroidered on it."

"No, *dummy*. In the *chair*." She pointed.

Sitting on a chair was a small dog looking up at me. It was Lauren.

"She looks so different." I didn't recognize her from the photograph.

"She's put on weight. She was supposed to," Amy defended her.

So I sat down and held Lauren in my arms and stroked her. Her coat looked bristly but was deceivingly soft. It was hot and Amy had no air conditioning, so we went outside to be in the breeze.

Still holding Lauren, I lay down next to Amy in the grass and looked up at the green trees against a hazy Virginia sky. As I smelled the grass and the earth, the leaves rustled above me. Lauren seemed content to lie on my stomach. At length, she hopped off, then started to run in circles.

"She's doing whirlies!" cried Amy in delight.

"What?"

"When she started to recuperate at the vets, they'd let her out and she'd run around and around. The vet techs called it 'the whirlies'."

"The whirlies," I stated in mock disgust. I hated corny phrases or when people baby-talked their animals. Then Lauren started playing with Bogie and Autumn. She'd bite them on the hock and wait for them to go after her. They played and played and finally they all collapsed panting on their sides.

"She's bad," Amy turned over on her stomach.

"What do mean?"

"When she was at the vets she tunneled into the other dogs' runs, looking for food. She could've been killed."

"She must be very smart."

"Nah!" Amy scoffed. "She was after food. She still thinks she's starving. You should've seen her when I first brought her home. She'd flail herself against the icebox. I'm not kidding."

"See, she's smart." I said and tried to picture a small dog flinging itself against a cold, white refrigerator in search of food, but could not.

"No, she just has a serious food fixation."

I watched Lauren now sniffing around in the grass. She wasn't mine, yet I felt bonded to her, I guess because I was supposed to have taken her. She looked healthy, yet she was far from well. When she was out of immediate danger of dying, the vets had started medicating her. They assumed she'd had distemper early in her life and it had caused her to have the seizures that she would now live with the rest of her life. Amy told me about them. To keep the seizures under control, she gave Lauren phenobarbital twice a day and administered a syringe of potassium bromide daily as well. Lauren still had the disease that had broken down her immune system, but there was no medication for that. She just had to live with it.

I was watching her when all of a sudden she flipped over on her back and started twisting. I leaped up and ran to her.

"Relax," Amy called. "It's not a seizure—she's just doing the squirmies."

"The whirlies, and now the squirmies. I'm going home." I said goodbye to my sister and her dogs, kissed Lauren atop her brown head, then hoped in my father's car.

Chapter 4

I found myself driving to Amy's almost every day. My form of therapy. She wasn't always there during the day, for she had to work, but I felt drawn. I went to see Lauren. I'd go inside and open the back door, and all the dogs would rush out in one crazy stampede. I knew each one of Amy's dogs could tell a story about my sister—why it had entered her life—that I didn't know; that I would never know, no matter how well I loved her or she loved me back. Amy's dogs were all big except Autumn, Bogie and Lauren. Lauren would wag her tail and when she did her whole body wagged with it. Then sometimes the tail made circles, like a propeller, a separate entity from the rest of her body. I let her march around under the big red maple and the plum trees. I watched her as she did the squirmies on her back in the sun: twist and twist and twist. She really did look as if she was having a seizure. Then I'd sit back in one of the two Adirondack chairs and wait till she hopped up on my lap, which she did within minutes of my sitting down. I'd hold her and stroke her, then put my head back and close my eyes and feel the sun on my face. Sometimes I'd fall fast asleep and dream I was back in the Luxembourg gardens. Then a dog would bark or Lauren's toenails would dig into me and I'd wake up. I had all kinds of thoughts as I sat there, but mostly I would just try to feel. I knew it felt good to have Lauren there on my lap, or just to watch her walking around or playing with Bogie and Autumn. I knew I was growing attached. On days when I couldn't go to see her, I felt an acute void. It was like nothing I'd ever felt before, like an addiction, I suppose. I remember when I first told Jason that I might be in love with him.

"I feel good when I'm near you, and better still when I talk to you. Follow that to its logical conclusion." I told him how it felt so right, but it didn't make sense because I knew something was wrong.

And he had quoted Pascal to me, "*Le Coeur à ses raisons que le raison ne connaît pas.* The heart has its reasons that the reason doesn't know." I wish now, as one always tends to do after the fact, that I'd retorted with another line from Pascal: "*Nous aimons à être trompés.* We loved to be deceived." But I hadn't understood then.

And I realize now that only in retrospect do we ever fully understand why someone or something enters or leaves our lives, and then sometimes not even in retrospect.

Chapter 5

It was all well and dandy reading novels, watching old movies, *I Love Lucy* reruns, and playing with Amy's dogs, but I knew I couldn't stay unemployed, becoming plumper by the minute with my mothers great dinners.

As the weeks passed, I thought of Jason less and less. As much of a cliché as it may sound, time does heal. In fact it's the only healer of which I know. Jumping into bed with someone else doesn't do the trick. Falling in love is great, but it has a funny way of not happening when you look for it, not happening till you're ready. Perhaps I was ready, but I didn't realize it. I did realize I needed to go out and find a job.

Not one to network, I got lucky. An old friend, Linda Beckford, invited Amy and me to dinner. Linda's father was editor of a prestigious review at the University of Virginia so I thought I'd take the opportunity to talk with him and see if he needed help. Linda stayed with her parents when home visiting from Manhattan. I brought Lauren; Amy brought Apache. The only thing Felicia Beckford, Linda's mother, loved more than horses was dogs.

I rang the bell, and Felicia's patrician presence greeted us.

"Hallo my loves! Do come in! And who have we here?"

"You remember Apache."

"And this is Lauren. We're trying to get her, uh, acclimatized."

"Well, aren't you just darling." Felicia stroked Lauren's head.

"Come in. Sit down. What would you like to drink?"

"Water," I answered.

"Co-cola for me," Amy said. We plopped down on the sofa. Amy settled Apache near her feet and he lay the evening there like a gentleman. At that moment Linda walked in.

"Hi y'all," she beamed. Linda was as beautiful as she was bright. Amy had taught her to ride and she'd then gone on to compete at

Madison Square Garden. Naturally as soon as Linda sat down next to Amy the talk turned to horses, and with horses and their respective owners, to scandal.

"So what's this I hear about Tessie Bud taking a younger lover?"

I let my mind drift for a minute. I settled Lauren on my lap and she turned her head around and gazed up at me.

"He was her yard boy."

"Gossip makes the world go round," sang Amy.

"It's all true. I was there when it happened." Linda defended her rumor.

"I believe you. She only ever talks about one thing."

"And that one thing is overrated," I said.

"Oh Kay, you're just smarting from getting over your poor little broken heart." Amy had no time for self-pity.

"Well it is," I insisted. "When you think that sex is as old as, or older than, the Blue Ridge Mountains to which we now look out...Rats, apes, we all do it..."

"Kay," Linda looked at me with a funny expression. "Have you ever been in *love*?"

Before I could answer our hostess called, signaling dinner was served, and we trooped in, drinks in hand, placing ourselves around the great Sheraton table. Conversation would, I knew, eventually get back to sex. It always did. At least in France it always did.

But since I knew Felicia had recently returned from the Keenland sales, I asked her about her trip to Kentucky, instead of asking her if she had good sex with her husband. Before she could respond, Linda chirped in a sing-song voice, "Lexington, Lexington, home of wide lawns and narrow minds."

"Do shut up dear. I know plenty of good minds in Lexington."

"You never brought them home to meet me. Hey, don't tell anyone but Mother bought a horse."

"What?" I was incredulous for these were potentially the best thoroughbreds in the world.

"Yup," Linda continued. "A gorgeous bay filly."

"Well I always said I know instantly when I like something. I was that way about your father after all." We all laughed as Felicia spoke up for herself, and I thought, okay, maybe now's the time to ask.

"I always know right away when I get on a horse," Amy stated and everyone turned towards her and listened. I'd missed my chance.

There was a tacit understanding in the local community that Amy was unequaled when it came to riding or breaking green horses. I always figured her talent arose from the fact that she was far more at home with animals than she was with humans. "I know immediately if I like it," Amy continued, "because unlike people, horses don't, or can't, hide their defects. They don't put on a nice act, or a sophisticated act, over dinner and then months later you find out the quirks. Horses are all right there up front when you first ride them. *You* might ruin them. You always run that risk."

What Amy said was true, and I suddenly became despondent thinking about the human race. I normally held a comic view of life that saw the beauty, the absurdity and the irreverence in any situation, but tonight I felt worried about where my own life was going. I guess the young worry, because they don't have the years to temper their personalities. The young also have no time for pondering mortality. The old know their time is limited and each new sunrise is accounted for and ticked off. I thought of Pascal Quignard's wonderful book and the line from which the title comes, *Tous les matins du monde sont sans retour*. All the mornings of the world are without return. *Sen vola via l'età*: The summer of life is fleeting. I thought about the question Linda had asked me. I was young, and I didn't want to die without ever having really loved someone.

Noticing my preoccupation and undoubtedly finding it rude not to be contributing to this colorful conversation, Felicia commented, "Your little one is very good, Kay."

Lauren was being good and I was amazed. She lay by my chair and didn't take her eyes off me.

All of a sudden there was a loud crash and we all jumped up and ran to the kitchen. There before us on the counter staring was a gray cat switching its tail from side to side. The Beckford's Waterford serving bowl lay upon the floor, treacle oozing out from it.

"Oh Dazzle, you've done it this time now, haven't you."

"Mother, you know that cat can't see. He's a hundred and nine years old."

"No, Linda, he does it for the attention. He doesn't like the canine strangers, to whom he's not been properly introduced, being here. But he's going to have to get used to it, aren't we Dazzle dear? Oh, Dazzle I didn't want to drag the dog guests upstairs and under the bed to introduce you. Come on, now." At that another crash sounded and Dazzle looked up in surprise. We rushed back to the dining room in time to see Lauren leap off the table with a look of triumph and glee in her eye. For a brief moment I had forgotten about her. She had knocked over a chair on her way up to the table and now, as she squirted off to the living room, I yelled,

"Lauren!"

Lower and lower to the ground she scuttled, but faster and faster, for she carried the entire pheasant in her mouth. I caught up with her, but the damage was done. Slobber and holes covered the remaining bird. I wrestled it out of her clamped teeth, and in my determination I didn't hear the hoots of laughter behind me. When I looked up, I saw Linda, Felicia and Amy doubled over.

At that moment Linda's father strolled in in tennis whites.

"Ladies... Sorry I'm a bit late."

"It's not a problem, dear. There's no dinner anyway."

Yet the dinner for me was a huge success. Besides realizing the extent of Lauren's eating disorder, I received a phone call from Bobby Beckford the following day. He knew I'd come back from Paris. For the fun of it, certainly not the money in it, Bobby circulated a monthly review of Paris, a little five-page affair, whose subscribers numbered probably no more that two hundred all in the same town. While the actual name of the newsletter was something else, to his friends Bobby called it, *The Poop on Paris*, which, in time, I altered further to *Paris Poop*. Bobby loved the city, having spent time there during the war, and wanted a reason to go back occasionally. But he couldn't return monthly or even bimonthly, nor did he want to. The review, which I think was in danger of folding when I came around, discussed politics and the arts. Bobby kept up with French politics from the States and wrote the political reviews. He needed a restaurant reviewer, film critic, museum and arts critic. Twist my arm. I said I'd take the job.

Chapter 6

While I was getting over Jason, I still missed him, or missed being with someone. I continued to think about being alone in that city, made specifically for all lovers in love. I thought about being alone in the places we'd been together, and about bumping into him and his wife. What would I do?

"Hi Jason's wife. I'm...." Never mind.

But I realized also that I secretly longed to bump into him and would probably spend each day of each year waiting for it to happen. Cities are big places, bigger still when you're waiting for the improbable to happen. It never does. Only the unexpected happens.

But the one thing I knew was that I didn't want to be alone again. I decided to talk to Amy.

"Of course I want to go back to Paris," I hollered at Amy, "but it's filled with memories."

We sat across from each other in a diner and I ate fried eggs with hash browns, while she ate waffles covered in butter and smothered in syrup.

"If I took Lauren with me, I wouldn't be lonely. I love her, you know that."

"I love her too. It's been over a year. Your statute runs out some time, you know. You can't just expect for me to give her up... she's part of the family now. She loves the country."

I didn't know what to say. I understood my sister, but I desperately loved and wanted that little dog.

"She'll have the country when she's here. I'll visit lots. I need the country too."

"Yeah, and she'll live in your cramped little apartment the rest of the time."

"But the difference now is that I'll be there with her. Anyhow, just think about it. I love her."

"Okay, I hear you. Don't beleaguer your point. It's not becoming."

"Belab—"

"Shut up Kay." She took a bite of soggy waffle. "You'd have to take care of her. You'd have to give her her drugs. You've never had a dog, you know, it's not that easy. You can't just hop on a plane to China like you like to do. You have a responsibility." My older sister lectured me.

"Don't you see, I *want* that. I need that. I'm ready." It was true. Because I'd lived in cities throughout my early adult life, I'd always felt it'd be unfair to have a pet, so I never got one. But this was different.

I'd been used to being completely free, completely spontaneous, no responsibilities. I would hop on planes and trains all the time and fly to exotic countries, seeking adventure—or perhaps seeking to fill my little life. Travel broadened my views, exposing my mind to different cultures, and I was certain I'd learned more from my travels to foreign places than I ever had in the classroom. I'd traveled Asia, South America, Africa and Europe extensively. As children, we'd traveled across our own nation with our family every summer. So I now felt I'd traveled enough and could settle down for a bit. I wanted this dog.

"I'll think it over," Amy ventured. "But don't go thinking she's yours. I said I'll *think* about it."

"Thank you."

I laid down a thirty percent tip.

"Spreading the wealth?"

"Spreading the wealth."

Amy caught sight of the Tasty Freeze across the street. I knew what was coming. She had atrocious eating habits and I lectured her constantly.

"Kay." She smiled at me.

"No. That stuff'll kill you."

"Like what we just had won't? Oh, come on," she wheedled.

"Let's not and say we did." I grabbed her arm and headed her to the car.

"You're boring and no fun at all." And she pouted all the way home.

That evening I knocked on her door, then handed her a giant bowl of Tapioca pudding. Her favorite, second to Tastee- Freez.

"Oh!" She cried in delight, grabbing it, and there's no doubt in my mind that she devoured the entire bowl that evening.

Chapter 7

A week before I was to go to Paris, I was in the kitchen at Amy's, when she called me to sit down on the sofa beside her. Lauren hopped up on my lap as I scrunched in between two salukis.

"You can take Lauren." Amy stroked Little Autumn. "But don't think you can take her, then give her back, or take her then give her to me while you go to Peru for six weeks," Amy sounded angry, but I knew it was just her manner. "If you take her, she's yours and you have to give her her drugs twice a day every day for the rest of her life, and deal with any medical problems that may come up... she's not an easy dog to care for... and you love her and you take care of her."

"I do love her." I looked at Lauren. *Forever.* I looked back up at Amy, feeling both moved and elated. "I will sis. Forever."

"Don't start that emotional crap on me," Amy turned her attention to Zsa Zsa.

"What made you decide to do it?"

"She cries every time you leave."

I stared again at Lauren, then leaned over and hugged Amy.

"Okay, okay, I have to go feed the horses."

"I'll help you."

"Damned cobwebs." She grabbed a broom and started batting the walls. "They're everywhere."

"Makes the place feel antique." I thought that comment amusing.

She didn't. "Just makes it feel dirty. Like I don't have enough dirt with fourteen dogs coming and going."

"How do they get there anyway?"

"Cobs, dummy."

And we walked outside laughing together. The air felt soft on my skin.

As we filled the scoops with grain Amy turned to me and asked, "Are you excited about your job then?"

"Yes, but I'll miss it here. The trees, the smells—"

"You're such a romantic."

"A romantic realist, which is better than a realistic romantic."

"Romantics bore me. No wonder you can never keep a relationship. When the romance is over and the hard work sets in…"

"Hey, wait a minute," I protested.

This time she smiled and put her arm around me, for she knew I'd never walked away from a relationship. We walked up the hill. The setting sun silhouetted the great maple. I inhaled the sweet summer air. So long Virginia. I was going back to Paris.

Chapter 8

Lauren was to go to Paris with me. The process was not as difficult as many people assumed, for the French love their dogs and have very lenient laws.

I went to the vets to get Lauren a health certificate, the first of many I would get for her over the years to come. She was in good enough health to travel. She was over the weight limit of seven kilos required if taking the dog into the cabin, but I ignored this fact for never would I place her or any dog in cargo. The conditions were erratic. The temperature could be either excessively hot or cold. The noise was loud. The animal would be all alone.

"And what if the plane crashes?" I howled at Amy. "I want to be *with* her."

"If the plane crashes you're dead and she's dead so it really doesn't matter, does it?"

My obsession with plane crashes began with that first flight with Lauren. I'd flown all over the world and never cared a lick. But now I had something to care about.

I bought a little baby carrier that I could put Lauren in and strap to myself. I'd seen kids being carried in these before. This was in case the plane crashed into water and we were asked to jump into life boats. I didn't want anyone telling me, "People first. No dogs." She would be attached to me. She would come with me or I would refuse to jump.

"If the plane goes down, you go get her. You call and you find her," I urged.

Amy made fun of my obsession, "If the plane goes down, you're *both* dead. What makes you think that Lauren is going to survive when you and everyone else perish in the flames?"

I just had this feeling that she would survive and nobody would know she was there.

As the years went by, my only worry was not that Lauren would die and leave me—I would deal with that when the time came because I loved her—but that I would be killed and she would have to live on alone, or with someone who didn't love her the way she was used to being loved, wondering all the time where I was and when I was coming back. Pets are different from children. We take care of children, but then they grow up and learn to take care of themselves, and we know we'll die, but they'll be okay to go on. Our pets, on the other hand, we care for throughout their lives. They're unquestionably smarter than we are, but we domesticate them, so that they become dependent on our care. As the fox so eloquently told the Little Prince, "You become responsible forever for the one you have tamed."

The day came for my departure. You'd think I would have grown tired of always being the one to say goodbye. I think it's part of our modern culture, in this age of jets and cars and trains. We have the capability to be able to leave, and to go farther than our ancestors did two hundred years ago. So I said goodbye to my mother and father and Amy. I had dinner with a few close friends the evening before. Then Ted drove me to Dulles airport.

As we pulled up to the terminal my brother looked over at me.

"You take care of yourself now. Take care of the weasel too."

"The weasel?"

"Yeah, take care of the weasel."

And somehow the name stuck. Lauren became known, particularly to me and to Ted, as "the weasel."

"But she's not like a weasel, a blood-thirsty killer," Amy insisted. "She's more like a possum, the way she waddles and scavenges for food. You ought to call her that."

Later on Ted gave her another name that Amy just devoured. After spending five weeks in Paris with me and with Lauren, he once described her as, "an extremely bizarre... and fortunately rare... life-form." Amy couldn't get enough of the expression and referred to her as my "life-form" or most often just my "form" while her animals were "dogs."

I bought Lauren a dog ticket, even though she'd be in the vented travel bag stowed under the seat before me. I put her in the bag, after letting her go to the bathroom. I had fed her breakfast and let her drink that morning, but not again. Fortunately I was flying Air France, for not only was it a direct flight, less time cooped-up for Lauren, but also the French treat their dogs better than their human compatriots. The staff on board was no exception. She had to remain in the bag under the seat for the *décollage* or take-off, but then, "rriiippp" I undid the zipper, her head poked out, and out she hopped onto my lap. Pop went the weasel.

"*Oooh, qu'est qu'il est beau,*" they cooed. The attention was flattering.

I was amazed on that first flight over to Paris. She had never done this before in her life, and yet she behaved like a veteran flyer.

"*Il est très sage.*"

"*Oui, elle est sage,*" I'd repeat. The words I was to hear over and over.

People walked by and touched her. A German woman, observing her for a long time, declared, "She is so kind to everyone."

I held her in my arms and she lay peacefully observing all the activity of an airplane, her eyes moving about, her head turning this way, then that.

When the meal arrived, however, I knew the wise thing to do was to return her to the small bag. The smells would drive her crazy—she was still completely irrational when it came to food—and I didn't want her to eat anything until we had landed.

The smells reached her in the bag, but finally she slept. I slept too.

Chapter 9

The plane touched down at Charles de Gaulle airport at 7:10 Paris time. The flight from west to east is shorter than east to west, the tail winds helping the plane along. I was glad that Lauren would soon be able to get out and walk around. When I felt the wheels jolt heavily, once or twice, on asphalt, I was, as always, very calm. Yet I experienced that quick sudden thrill and familiar feeling of coming home. Only this time it was different. This time I felt different.

I grabbed a trolley, put Lauren's bag on top near my hands and opened it. Her head came out and she looked bleary-eye, but again she stayed quiet, remaining in the bag with no struggling, merely observing the passengers pushing carts, as if she understood the process. Perhaps she did—or perhaps she knew I did, felt my calm and reacted to that. As I wheeled her along towards the luggage belt, I felt the looks and glances. Kids rushed up to stroke her.

"*Mama, régard!*"

"*Oui, cherie, c'est un beau chien.*"

Questions from Americans:

"Oh, I didn't know you could bring a dog on the plane. Oh Bill, look, you can bring a dog on the plane. Tuffy would love to come. We have a two-year old cocker spaniel. Oh, she's so good. What's her name?"

And the explanations of how it worked and what was necessary in order to fly with your dog aboard plane went on. I really think the only thing necessary was to have a dog you love and a dog who trusts you, then that dog will be good.

I knew Lauren would be good before I went, though was every reason why she should not have behaved well, but I believed in her. She trusted me. And from that grew the strength of my relationship with this odd little dog. I respected her and, while I frequently laughed at her, I never did anything that would insult or damage her dignity.

I leaned down and kissed her on top of her brown head, raising my eyes back up in time to catch the most vicious scowl from a man not four feet away. The French were dog lovers. The Algerians were not. I had placed my lips on one of the most dirty creatures in Allah's kingdom. I shivered, for in his look I felt the power to kill. For a moment I was unnerved, then I reasoned: If he chose to live in France, then he had to abide by the French and their fancies. Just as I would abide by the North African customs were I to travel to Algeria or Tunisia. Certainly I would not kiss Lauren in public there.

The taxi zipped along past the ugly suburbs of Paris. The *banlieu-rouge* as much of it was called. In America, most crime occurs in the inner-city ghettos, but Paris is the opposite. The city herself remains remarkably safe. Although I'd heard stories to the contrary, I was never attacked or harassed walking the streets alone late at night. Certain métro stations—Les Halles, Barbès, La Chapelle—were less desirable after dark, but otherwise crime was dismissed to the suburbs, where it was commonplace. One reason for this was the large drug trade that went on in the *banlieu* and *bidonvilles*.

I often wondered how visitors to Paris would receive their first impressions when they came by taxi via the suburbs, for really there was no other way except the RER, the high-speed métro. How modern, when Paris was supposed to be ancient. How ugly, when Paris was supposed to be romantic and beautiful, the City of Light. And yet I felt drawn to these somber edifices for they were in fact the essence of France. These were just as much a part of her culture as the baroque churches and neo-classical buildings. Then as if challenging my thoughts, rising out in the distance I spied the onion domes of Sacré-Coeur, offering me a hint of the wondrous city awaiting.

As we entered Paris' city limits, my heart beat faster. We drove along the quai de Bercy and the quai de la Rapée, crossing the Seine on the pont d'Austerlitz. Many of France's streets and bridges are named after famous battles or famous people, and when leading visitors from the States around Paris, I always appeared particularly intelligent as I explained to them after whom or what each street was named. What they never knew was that I merely had good eyesight. The streets and boulevards of Paris are marked exceptionally well, with blue plaques, which in most cases tell not only the name, but in smaller letters beneath, the respective dates of that person's life and what he or she did. I believed history should be made accessible to the vast public and not something one could only discover leafing through dust-covered pages in the archives, however much I did enjoy those dusty archives.

Lauren was partially in her bag and sound asleep. I nudged her.

"Look Lauren, there's Notre Dame." I said it quietly. The sun coming up over the buildings in the east touched the apse of the great gothic cathedral which, with its radiant flying buttresses, appeared feather-light and ready to embark from its island amidst the river. It would, however, remain standing solid as it had done for nearly one thousand years. And tourists from all over the world would come to behold Our Lady. They would crowd into her nave and turn to stare at the great indigo Rose window; they would crowd in during Sunday evening organ concerts to marvel at the acoustics; they would stand before her and snap photos; and they would climb the two hundred and sixty some steps (I had once counted) to the first level to stand face to face with the gargoyles, wave at the less ambitious below, and maybe meet the hunchback. Then on a hundred and some more steps to the very top. Although I think the top became a favorite and romantic spot for suicides and it had to be closed.

I'd seen Notre Dame de Paris from this view a hundred or more times and it still gave me chills. I looked at my arm, sure enough. I looked at Lauren. Sure enough, asleep again. Paris, big deal.

We drove past the Jardin des Plantes, then up the rue Lacépède, stopping on the Place de la Contrescarpe.

"OK Lauren, let's go." I snapped the leash on her and let her jump out of the taxi, her paws touching the cobblestones of the Paris streets for the first time. She did a big stretch right in the middle of the road as two mopeds swerved to avoid her. I jumped to her rescue, and paid the driver, who charged for every bag carried and of course for *le chien*. I let Lauren go to the bathroom then carried the bags up the short flight of steps to the apartment.

It always smelled the same, a little musty. I glanced up; the books were all there on the bookshelves. Lauren was sniffing around exploring her new lodgings. I inhaled deeply then opened the windows wide.

How the sounds of the outside and of the streets came to life with the opening of a window. From the café directly below, the talk, the laughter, the clink of glasses rose up to greet me. I shivered. Sun-warmed air filtered in. There were two more cafés that bordered the square, one across from me and one to the side. Each café attracted a distinct and different Parisian crowd, but the tourists went to whichever had more sun. The square itself was lovely and green with four Polonia trees, seasonal flowers and a fountain that splashed its melodious song from nine in the morning till midnight. Surrounding the grassy square and fountain, the rose granite cobblestones were worn by wear, then replaced, worn again, and replaced, with time-honored reliability.

The place de la Contrescarpe hadn't always been so enchanting, however. Pick up any guidebook from the past and the square is alternately described as seedy or disreputable. The fountain was added only recently. The noise from the construction drove me to distraction and I'd leave my desk and walk other neighborhoods for hours. Before, *the place* had been just a raised bit of pavement like a sidewalk, but in a square shape, and here the *clochards* or tramps had congregated. Pick up *The Sun Also Rises* or *A Moveable Feast*, and you'll find these same bums. They are not, however, like the guys sleeping on the métro benches. They are cultured tramps and I knew each one. They were still there, same as they were in Hemingway's time and before, although they disliked the beautification of the square, mostly because the fountain splashed over its railing and got them wet while they slept.

As I stood gazing out, I saw no *clochards*, just couples strolling and holding hands. The sun slipped in and out from behind puffy cumulus clouds. I looked down the rue Cardinal Lemoine and could see number 74 where Hemingway had lived in his youth, with his wife Hadley.

"That's the *only* reason you got that apartment. You can't fool anyone Kay," Amy said. Well, it wasn't the only reason, but I did like having Hemingway's ghost around the corner.

It was still morning and I knew if I let myself sit I'd sleep, and since I wanted to get my body on Paris time, I should stay awake and simply go to bed early. I unpacked my bags quickly, made a note to call the French vet whose name I'd been given, then called Lauren. She was curled up sleeping on my sofa, the air from the open window gently blowing her ruff.

"Let's go!"

She hopped down and stood waiting before the door. I clipped on the long extension leash I'd bought for her, and we walked out into the dark hallway, down the steps and out into welcoming bright sunlight.

And so my life with Lauren in Paris had begun. I knew where we were going, where I always went first. I wanted to show Lauren the Luxembourg Gardens. She trotted up ahead, at the end of the long, black leash, stopping frequently to sniff where male dogs had left their mark. She behaved as if she'd walked the history laden streets of Paris many times in her life. She didn't look up at the grandeur of the Pantheon when we passed it. She just trotted along, nose to the ground.

I had to be ever observant, however, as I controlled her diet because of her health. Naturally I didn't want her eating greasy French fries or discarded pieces of pastry from the gutters. Whenever I spied a half-eaten sandwich ahead in our path before she did, I'd quickly pull her up short making a detour, or else she'd seize it, gulping it down without chewing as she marched her way through the streets.

She loved food more than any creature I've ever known. That part about her never changed. Only the times when she was gravely sick did she lack her tremendous and tireless appetite. Amy said at least I'd know for certain when to do it. In other words, if Lauren ever lost her desire for food, it would signal the time to end her life, for food was her reason for living.

Sometimes when out walking the streets of Paris Lauren would glimpse a flock of pigeons. She'd break from her normal pace and run after them! Hunting dog, beagle, she wanted to attack the birds, her instinct, right? Wrong. Scavenger. Lauren knew a flock of pigeons meant bread crumbs or a *demi-baguette*. She'd charge the doves, and they'd scatter, flapping and fluttering disconcertedly above my head, leaving the mess of food all for Lauren. She couldn't have cared less about the birds themselves. I just laughed and laughed and rarely let her have the garbage she'd so smartly sought out.

On this day I avoided the busy corner of the rue Soufflot and the blvd. St-Michel where *MacDoes* sat. I didn't want to risk Lauren getting trod on, and of course French fries littered the streets there. We took the back streets, past the Chinese grocery and the Crédit Lyonnaise, to where before us rose the black iron gates of the Luxembourg Gardens. My heart jumped as it always did, and has always since, upon seeing the gardens for the first time after being away. Waiting at the edge of the busy boulevard, I watched until the little red man on the signpost turned green. Lauren trotted right beside me, and then triumphant, in we marched through the gates. I let her leash out long and off she went stopping at each chestnut tree we passed.

The part of the gardens in which I was walking allowed dogs. You saw lots of them, with an assortment of owners. It was a great way to meet people, and in the years to come I would find that Lauren was a magnet for beautiful French women. They found her intriguing, I guess because she was different from their Yorkies and poodles. Because I'd always seen dogs here, I assumed they were permitted in all sections of the gardens. This, however, was not the case, as I would soon find out. This fact was clearly posted, but never having had a dog, I'd paid the signs little attention. Dogs for that matter were welcome in very few parks in Paris. I never understood why. Weren't the parks better places for dogs than the streets? I guess it was to protect small children from stepping in dog messes.

We walked along, me stopping and waiting for Lauren as she met other dogs, sniffing them directly, while I smiled at the owners. We passed children running and lovers holding hands, students reading and absorbing rays of sunshine. I looked over at the palace built by Salomon de Brosse for Marie de' Medici in the seventeenth century. I looked over to the unequal towers of St-Sulpice behind it. I looked to the statue of Marie herself, stern and forbidding. I looked to the many statues, David, Calliope, Flaubert and Stendhal, who watched over the gardens day in, day out. I looked at the multitude of shapes and colors of flowers carefully and precisely planted around the green grass. And all around me I saw the French insouciantly living their individual lives. I was here, I was in Paris. I was standing in this place that I loved, this garden that I cherished, and I was not alone. I looked over to the school children laughing and playing in the grass and I too laughed out loud. I looked down and Lauren's brown eyes stared back up at me as if to say,

"What are we stopping for?"

"OK let's go." Lack of sleep was beginning to catch up with me, but I continued.

As I went I realized I was, without thinking, walking to work. It was automatic. I paused. Jason was still in my mind, but he'd become a log floating down a distant river. He would probably always be floating, but he would float farther and farther away from me.

"What the heck," I said to myself. I wanted to share with Lauren all the places I loved.

Then, occurring simultaneously with my thought process, a whistle sounded sharply. Turning toward the piercing sound, I saw a guard walking pointedly toward me and waving his stick at Lauren.

"*Mademoiselle! Pas des chiens! C'est interdit.*"

"*Ah bon? C'est interdit?*" While in the years to come as this event happened over and over I would feign ignorance and put on my most atrocious American accent, which wasn't at all hard to do, this time I really was oblivious to the rule.

"*Oui Mademoiselle. La bas seulement.*" And he directed me to the part of the park from where we had just come.

"*Excusez-nous.*" I retreated, pulling the illegal beagle along. So we strolled back the way we'd had come, but in future attempts Lauren and I would walk in the forbidden areas, my eyes always alert for the *gendarmes*. It elicited the same thrill as doing something forbidden as a kid. When I would hear the familiar shrill piercing blow of the whistle I would walk as though I were preoccupied, and I swear Lauren likewise would adopt a very guileless air about her.

On the way back to the apartment, Lauren decided to stride up to every restaurant, all now open and serving lunch, and proceed in through the door. Her long leash allowed it as I watched from the sidewalk outside. Diners smiled in amusement and the waiters, complicit to her prank, called her forth.

"Come on, Lauren. Let's go home." She turned her head and gazed forlornly back at me as if to say, "You never feed me." And did I ever feel guilty. She pulled this trick frequently and won the hearts of everyone around her, while I received wicked glares.

I did always feed her. It was the happiest time of day for her and oh, so short-lived. She gulped down her food without, I believe, really tasting it, faster than any dog I'd ever seen—a small vacuum that ran without batteries. I came to cherish the chomping noises she made while she ate, her tail sticking straight out behind her. The feeding hour became known as "the Feeding Frenzy." I dubbed it this one day at Amy's when the dogs, Lauren in particular, were terribly excited in expectation of food. From then on I'd always yell out "Feeding Frenzy!" and Amy would get mad and say I got them all the more riled up. But it stuck and every evening before feeding Lauren I'd ask, "Well, do you know what time it is?" Then, when her ears pricked, I'd respond in the highest-pitched tone I could bring forth, "it's a Feeding Frenzy!" As time went on all I had to say was, "It's a...." very softly and Lauren would leap up from wherever she was and come running. And finally, I could but look at her and whisper, "Well..." and she knew the rest. She'd hop, hop, hop up and down and pace the floor as I filled her bowl. She'd tremble and shake, and if I told her to stop shaking, she'd shake more. She'd snap her mouth at me noiselessly, as if to say, "Hurry up." And it didn't take long to identify the odd, rattling sound I heard as I stood at the counter filling her food bowl: her teeth chattering in the anticipation of the meal.

That evening I did the Feeding Frenzy for the first time in Paris. It didn't really matter to Lauren, though—just as long as she got fed. I disguised her pills in bits of dog food. She hated the syringe, but accepted it each time solemnly. I cooked fried eggs and French green beans for myself and went to bed early. Lauren slept next to me, her head on one pillow, mine on the other.

Chapter 10

I woke to the sounds of the street cleaners, dressed in their ecological green, washing, brushing and scraping clean the city with their matching green brooms. I have always smiled in appreciation at them, for the city remains beautiful and one of the cleanest I know largely due to their efforts.

I rolled over and said good morning to Lauren half asleep beside me. I wondered how many mornings, before Amy had found her, she would have woken only to be scared, wary and hungry.

One of the first things I observed while living with her was how often she would lie upside down, hind legs splayed out, and front legs straight up in the air. Even long after she'd fallen asleep the front legs remained stuck up in the air, as if rigor mortis had set in. I couldn't figure it out. Then sometimes, one of the front legs would fold over and begin to flap. Amy explained it to me as the "flapping leg syndrome." I thanked her for her help. Amy also told me that Lauren easily won the Road Kill Contest. I found out why when I observed her asleep, upside down, eyes rolled back into her head, white, and mouth open showing teeth and tongue.

"Lauren, I've never seen a lovelier dog in all my life."

Eyes rolled slightly to look at me, then rolled back up into her head again.

"That's really pretty, Lauren."

The second thing I observed was, when she wasn't doing road kill imitations, she'd either lie with her hind legs straight out like a frog, or with her front legs tucked under her like an amputee dog. While each pose was equally cute, and she garnered a lot of attention this way, I'm certain she did neither with any motivation in mind.

Well rested, I was ready to show the weasel the city I loved. It was September. *La Rentreé*. The city wakes up from the sleepy summer, and each day the streets fill a little more with people returning from *le midi*, and more and more shops open.

We started off on the rue Rollin, the gutters running with water as they always did in the morning. To the east the sky blushed peach and the air was suffused with that ineluctable Parisian smell, that is, but is also much more than, *café au lait* and baking *baguettes*. Over the years I had seen many dogs walk this small dead-end street and I figured it'd be a good place for Lauren to go to the bathroom.

Sure enough, after sniffing several bollards, she squatted down. When she did, she always raised the left hind foot—not high in the air the way male dogs do—but very daintily, an inch from the ground so as not to get wet. Ted, however, when he visited, insisted that this act of hers might save one foot, but the rest did not escape, and he started calling her "Tinkle Toes."

Ted's teasing aside, Lauren became very good about going to the bathroom in the city, an altogether different experience when you're used to the soft permeable grass of the country.

Next came the more solid part of the bathroom exercise. In the country you merely let your dog outside and assume he does what's intended of him. There's not the concern that you perforce have in the city.

I soon learned that while Paris had more dog lovers per capita than anywhere else, there were certainly those who did not share our enthusiasm. This was primarily due to the fact that very few Parisians cleaned up after their pooches the way they did in New York, for example. True they were supposed to, just as they were supposed to have their dogs go in the gutters. There were even arrows with white dachshunds pointing to the streets lest owners feign forgetfulness—but these evidently went unobserved. I guess dog owners thought, "Why bother," when the *motocrots* would be coming by later. The *motocrots* were motorcycles with long vacuum tubes that sucked up each dog's *crot*. Ah Paris.

Lauren started to squat down again, but in a different way from before that signaled something else. Feeling like a torturer, I dragged her over a little so not to be right before a doorway. Nor was she in the middle of the pedestrian street, so I assumed all was OK.

But oh, no. Around the corner, out of nowhere, came a woman *d'un certain âge*, speaking rapid French that I could only translate as:

"Mademoiselle, it's because of you and your dogs that there's dog poop all over the city! You're disgusting Mademoiselle as much as your dog is because you let it to poop! If it cannot go where it is told, it should not poop. No, it should not poop!"

She didn't leave me a moment to respond, "Dear Madame, I shall gladly pick up my dog's poop if it would make your day and world a better one." I don't think she wanted me to respond; she only wanted to air her grievances, which probably included her son or grandchild not getting into l'ENA, the Ecole Nationale d'Administration as she'd dreamed, her husband's general neglect of her, her body's natural aging process and so on. Lauren and I were the targets. I think she felt better.

I left Lauren's offending material where it was—beside the building where Descartes had lived—and rethought the name of the newsletter. *The Dog Poop in Paris*. Descartes had deemed animals soulless machines, without feeling. Here's to you, Descartes.

As one might expect Paris is teeming with history. I loved walking the cobblestone streets and imagining that Voltaire and Mirabeau and Mme. de Sévigné had walked these very steps of mine. Even an unassuming, out of the way street like the rue Rollin, could boast to famous dwellers. As well as the blue signs, naming each street, there were also wonderful plaques describing who lived where and had done what. We walked by number 2, rue Rollin where Pascal had died on the 19th of August 1662 at his sister's. At number 4, in a building begun in 1623, had lived Bernardin de Saint-Pierre who wrote the love story *Paul et Virginie*. Number 8 was were Rollin himself, writer and rector of a university, lived and died. And number 14 boasted to having Descartes' presence for a while. The French owe much to Descartes, for the soul of French society is fundamentally Cartesian.

The rue Rollin is a curious street for it dead-ends into two steep stairways that descend to the rue Monge, and during the warm months, the space between the steps is planted with cascading flowers. Down we went and turned right on the rue Monge and walked along the busy street until reaching the place Monge with its bustling market. In the distance I heard church bells ringing.

The marché Monge, a roving market held only three mornings a week, differs from the quotidian street market in this respect and that the produce tends to be from local growers. I walked by piles of fresh peaches, the last of the season. The figs would soon be coming in. I inhaled the briny smell of the olives and was transported to the cours Saleya market in Nice. I don't know how this happened but it never failed to work—if only for a few seconds in time. The *charcuterie* was arranged so neatly that I stopped to admire the *saucission d'Auvergne* and beautiful *patés*. The markets symbolized a way of life I could understand, basic, tangible and real, so far removed from the high-technological advancements that were happening every day, every minute, in virtually every field all in the name of progress. I realized that within the next ten years we would see the way we conducted commerce change drastically. But I was loath not only to step into the future, but even to catch up within the present. I hated email, and believed the internet would eventually destroy society as we knew it. So we received information faster, but at what price? The loss of individual contact, the thread that held us together and made us human. The internet itself does not create these conditions, but the solipsistic mentality that encourages it, or that it encourages, does. At this rate we were headed toward social isolation, toward cosmic entropy.

The street markets were antithetical to the information highways. They were inordinately labor intensive, with the putting up and taking down of each stand at the beginning and end of each day. Yet every *vendeur* was intensely proud of his *métier* and arranged his fruits or vegetables with loving pride. Every *vendeur* also understood and realized the value of what he did. I wondered if the guys somewhere in the middle of the banking pyramid even knew why they did what they did. They only knew they made money. Lots of money. Paper money. But was it real? Corn and wheat are real. Peaches and plums are real. I have always opted for a barter system, because it makes more sense to me. The market life made sense to me. So too do animals' lives. They eat when hungry, drink when thirsty and sleep when tired; they are dictated by their bodies' natural rhythms. What a luxury that seems in our high-tech world.

Waiting in line for leeks I listened to the different languages. I loved the black skin of the Senegalese next to the flaxen hair of the Norwegian. I admired the last of the red strawberries piled high next to the *pêches de vignes* and the blood oranges, with their shockingly red, but delicious, interiors. Beside them were the tiny green *Reine Claude* plums. Yes, Paris was a moveable feast.

Leaving the place Monge market we walked down the rue Gracieuse, turned right on the rue de l'Epée-de-Bois, then left on the rue des Patriarches. I was taking the back route to one of the most famous and colorful markets in Paris, the rue Mouffetard. We started at the bottom and worked our way up. Lauren was in dog heaven, or dog frustration, for aromas of food permeated the market: chickens, ducks and rabbits roasted on open spits, while potatoes baked below; the salty smell of the fish stalls; the pungent smell of cheese. Tidbits and scraps of food fallen in the street were in no short supply either.

At the foot of the rue Mouffetard was a spritely fountain and the church of St-Médard. The church was not as old as some, in other words, begun in the mid-fifteenth century instead of the tenth or eleventh. Its patron, St-Médard, originated the custom of delivering a wreath of roses to maidens whose conduct remained virtuous. But the church was primarily known for the convulsionists. In the early eighteenth century a Jansenist clergyman of saintly reputation, died at a young age of mortification of the flesh and was buried next to the church. Sick Jansenists came to the site to lie upon the grave and be cured, which led to mammoth demonstrations of collective hysteria. In 1732 Louis XV decided to put an end to such scenes and closed the cemetery. The inscription nailed to the gate translated to:

> *By order of the King, let God*
> *No miracle perform in this place!*

Alas, the convulsionists are long gone, and I'd rather not reflect upon what contemporary society offers in their place. Like many churches, St-Médard regularly held classical concerts, and I always tried to attend as many as possible. Neither Sunday, nor evening, there was no service or concert on this day, yet the doors were open and a few tourists strolled around the nave reading their green Michelin guides.

I picked Lauren up into my arms and walked in.

Immediately the air temperature changed as I entered through the doors. I sat down in one of the small wooden chairs and automatically looked straight ahead. I loved churches, particularly the romanesque. I didn't care the faith, although in France the majority are Catholic. Cistercian churches were my favorites. The Cistercians built their shrines on isolated sites with the most natural beauty, and believed in purity through austerity. Entering these sacred and pure dwellings always took me away from my petty problems and made me think. I stroked Lauren's head and ears. This warm, fury body on my lap was so trusting of my actions. She didn't worry that perhaps she was not allowed in the holy building, that there were forms of life discriminated against in our faith. No, she trusted me, and lay peacefully across my legs. Do animals believe? What need to believe or invent religions like we, when one simply *is*.

I pondered the destructiveness of religion over the ages and the continuation of it today. All in the name of God. We could learn so much from our animals. Belief is necessary, but rigid belief throws us off course. I preferred faith, and a faith that included doubt, as opposed to dogmatic belief. We were given minds after all to question what teachers or religions tell us is truth. If we have faith, we will trust our minds and not betray them by trying to believe what makes no sense to our heart and soul. Animals don't reason (or so I'm told), but they act on an instinct much like our faith.

Suddenly I'd had enough of the dark interior and craved the color and breath of the marché Mouffetard. I glanced around furtively, but no clergy were in sight. I rose, Lauren still in my arms, then paused for a brief moment. It was the first of many churches I would experience with Lauren, our favorite always the romanesque St-Germain-des-Pres, with all those tiny gold stars against blue.

The rue Mouffetard was crowded and vibrant with life. *Vendeurs* hollered and hawked their goods with enthusiasm and pride. I think you could find any food item you desired here, from the beautiful glistening oysters, divided into two categories, *creuses* and *plates*, and the jumbo tunas with gleaming red flesh, to the immense wheels of Emmental and perfectly formed logs of Montrachet. The redolence of newly baked bread was a treat for the nose as the vision of perfect pastries in pristine shop windows, or bunches of irises next to yellow tulips, was for the eyes. The market is an important and essential part of French life. To understand the French completely, you had first to understand the ritual of the market and the passion for food. For this is the true fabric of French society. The French still market daily, selecting just the right Camembert and flan for a meal mere hours away.

Up and up the steep cobblestone street Lauren and I ambled, stopping at the *crêpe* stand to buy a sugar and butter *crêpe*, until we reached the top and the place de la Contrescarpe.

"Come on Lauren," I called for she was foraging in the gutter after some bread crumbs. I tugged gently on the leash and as I looked back up, from around the corner of my building loped a large, handsome husky, German shepherd mix. It was headed directly towards Lauren. Lauren's back was to the dog as she rummaged along the curb, and it trotted right up to her, then stood stock still. Lauren must have finally sensed his presence for she whirled around, wary. They sniffed each other, and then the tails began to wag excitedly. Lauren crouched down, her haunches up in the air, and the silver shepherd made a bound in her direction. She jumped after him and he darted playfully down the street. Lauren flew after him quick as a rabbit, but when she reached the end of the long leash, she jerked abruptly backwards and did a small flip in the air. I ran to her, but she was off again playing with her new friend. More than once we came perilously close to tripping up a pedestrian who got between us, the long leash a hazard to anyone walking by. But Lauren was oblivious to the fact that she'd become a viable street hazard. Around and around they leaped after each other, until finally I had to call my dog to stop. She was reluctant, but I pulled her along, while she kept turning back to look.

On the square standing next to the fountain, ranting at a passerby, was Roland. I hadn't seen him since I'd returned and I was filled with genuine emotion.

"*Eh Voilà, Kay,*" he pronounced my name "Key."

I embraced this big burly and dreadfully smelly man. He was the ring leader of all the *clochards*. He lived outside on the square, and everyone in the neighborhood, from the most respectable to the least, called him the *chef de la place*.

"*Salut Roland, comment va tu?*"

"*Eh bah, je suis toujours là,*" he laughed and I laughed with him. Then curious, I asked him to whom the beautiful dog belonged, for it was evidently running loose.

"*Ah! C'est Jimmy, beau, n'est-pas?*"

"*Jimmy?*" An American dog in Paris. No, just an American name, named for James Dean. Another movie-star dog.

"*C'est le chien de Monsieur Bricarde,*" and he pointed down the rue Mouffetard to the Tunisian take-out. I told him I was glad to see him and he welcomed me back to his *place*. And so it was that Lauren had a new friend. His name was Jimmy.

Chapter 11

I quickly fell into a routine of writing my reviews in the morning about the restaurant I had dined in, the art exhibition I'd seen, or the film I'd watched the night before. Usually I went to the movies at Odéon on the left bank for, from my apartment, I could walk there in fifteen minutes, ten if I hurried. There were three mainstream cinemas at Odéon, and several other smaller ones. All the big films came to one of the three. The first film I was to review was the latest Berri film. I left Lauren alone in the apartment, and worried about her constantly throughout the movie, so much so that it greatly affected my feeling for the film. I'm not sure what I was afraid of, after all it was only for a matter of hours. But I guess my dramatic side took over and I started worrying about bombs going off in the cinema as it was a time of terrorism and many bombs. I can still hear Amy's gleeful laugh when I told her my latest train of thought and that I was counting on her to again rescue Lauren should I die, this time not from a plane crash, but from a bomb blast.

I decided to carry on me always in my wallet or in my *carte orange* a slip of paper that read on the outside: "*En urgence,*" or Emergency. Inside would read, "In case of death, I have a little dog all alone in my apartment. She takes medication. Please call 1-804-295-1722," Amy's number, "and say that Lauren is all alone in the apartment." I made the mistake of showing this paper to my sister once and she laughed so hard I really did think she was going to have a stroke. Folded up with the note I also enclosed a fifty franc note, so whoever retrieved the paper would have enough money to call the United States. I still have that paper. I still have the fifty francs that went with it, even though, replaced by the euro, the franc is now sadly obsolete.

I left the cinema in an agitated state, was assaulted by throngs of people waiting to see the next showing, and ran all the way home. I flung open the apartment door and there she was lying supine, white chest and tummy exposed, tail thumping in happiness, ears turned inside out in submission. I rubbed her stomach and kissed her as if I hadn't seen her in weeks. How many times had I returned to this apartment only to find it empty and myself still alone?

Not until I raised my head from her, though, did I notice for the first time Lauren's new arrangement of my apartment: The chair at my desk knocked over. The papers and books on the desk scattered all over the floor. The garbage can in the kitchen turned over, with debris strewn over the kitchen floor and out into the living room. I turned and looked at Lauren.

"What happened?"

Her ears turned even more inside out. She groveled at my feet, then flipped over on her back again. I never scolded her, just cleaned up the mess and tried to ignore her. That didn't last long.

When I told Amy about it, she explained that dogs get upset when we leave them, "especially when you smother them with love the way you do the life-form." She said that my worrying about Lauren so much at the movie probably communicated itself to my dog. I was doubtful, but I did know that dogs think in images and are much more sensitive and telepathic than we are. As for the trash can, well, I knew the temptation of food would always be stronger than the fear of any scolding or the hope of powerful praise. From that day forward I always put any garbage can up on the counter if I had to go out. If I didn't the outcome was predictable. Her obsession with food did lessen with the years. At the start, I believe, she really did think she was still starving. As time went by, however, she began to understand that I would always feed her—perhaps not as frequently or as much as she wished, but I always would.

Lauren was no needy, neurotic dog (aside from a small vacuum cleaner phobia, but I learned this was not uncommon in dogs or, I should add, in some humans.) However, I could read panic in her eyes if I left her alone in strange places. If I had to run into a grocery store, I'd tie her outside and she'd stare at the doorway, the place she'd last seen me. When she'd first glimpse me coming back, her ears would lie back and she'd either roll over in obeisance or she'd bounce up and down like she did before being fed.

When I had to leave the apartment, I'd leave bones or rawhides for her, but she wouldn't chew. She would instead lie by the door on the floor and wait for my footfall in the hall. When the neighbors said she howled, I had to believe them, though I found it difficult. She rarely barked in my presence.

Thus my decision to take Lauren to the movies with me was a direct result of both our separation anxieties. We walked together over the familiar streets to Odéon—down the rue de l'Ecole de Médecine, past the Viennese pâtisserie on the right; past the house with the beautiful loggia and the house where Charlotte Corday stabbed Marat in his bath; past Paris VI and the Université René Descartes (Paris V) and the statue of Bichat, the eighteenth-century anatomist—Lauren's travel bag slung over my shoulder, empty.

A block away from the cinema, I stopped, unzipped the bag and, in the middle of the sidewalk, gathered her into my arms and slipped her in. I put the bag once more over my shoulder, in an effortless way so no one would suspect live cargo, although it was now heavy with dog. Once in the movie house, I waited till the lights were dimmed and the *séances*, or advertisements, were finished to unzip the bag and let her out. I didn't know how this would go, but her behavior was exemplary. She slept on my lap for part of the film and then hopped off and stretched out in the aisle. I heard the jingling of her tags at one point during the movie and looked over to see her doing the squirmies in the middle of the carpeted walkway. She stopped and lay upside down, legs all spread out until a young man with a drink in each hand nearly tripped over her, walking down to his seat. But it didn't daunt her, for she just flopped over on her side and slept till the film finished.

We became quite adept at sneaking into the movies and I certainly think she preferred being there with me to being alone. These jaunts to the movies, however, were not trouble free. During a film, staring Isabelle Adjani, that I particularly wanted to see, Lauren would not behave. She refused to sit still and her rattling dog tags were beginning to disturb the audience. Heads turned around, as they will, to stare at me and nonverbally say, "Do something about it!" I didn't blame them, so I scooped her up and held her snugly on my lap.

It was only after the film ended, when the lights came back on, and the people luckily had forgotten about the earlier commotion, that I noticed the source of Lauren's agitation. There under the seat before me were two or three kernels of popcorn.

As I said it was a time of bombs in Paris. The possibility of one going off on the métro was always in the recesses of peoples' minds. When the bomb exploded in front of Tati, Paris' equivalent to K-mart, nobody felt safe. One could understand why the terrorists would target the foreign embassies, but why strike the working-man's domain? It was doubly confusing since the bombs were most often credited as the doings of the Islamic fundamentalists. Tati was where the North Africans shopped. The bomb killed their brothers, not the Americans or the wealthy French. When that bomb went off on the rue de Rennes I was one block from it. Walking past Tati and that blood-stained spot would forever fill me with an eerie feeling.

Thus, all the museums and public buildings routinely had bag checks when people entered. The CGT, machine guns tucked in their armpits, and the regular French police were more visible than ever, particularly around government buildings, like the Palais de Justice, the Préfecture de Police or the American Embassy.

I should not have been surprised, then, when I walked up and handed my ticket to a collector at the UGC cinema and he politely asked to look in my bag.

"Uh," I stammered, then shut up. *Ruat caelum.* Come what may.

I set the bag down and unzipped it. Of course, a furry brown head poked itself out with importance and there was my dog, strictly forbidden in the movie house. But then, this was France. The attendant smiled a big, toothy smile at me and bent down to touch Lauren. Keep her quiet, he said, and told me to go on in.

She never did watch one film.

Chapter 12

Shortly after I'd begun work for my new job, I got a phone call. "Hello?"

"I'm coming over." It was my brother, Ted. He'd been discussing the possibility of taking some time off to spend with me in Paris, and now it was definite. I was delighted.

"Okay, see you a week from tomorrow," I said.

"Right. Hey, how's the weasel doing over there?"

"She's great. You'll see."

"Yeah?" He sounded doubtful. "Her bark have an accent?"

"Huh?"

"Is she speaking French yet?"

"Understands. Doesn't speak."

"Well, there's still time. I'll see you soon."

Ted arrived on a beautiful crisp October morning. Lauren and I met him at Charles de Gaulle and we all three jumped in a taxi for Paris. Ted loved Paris as much as I did. He appreciated the city's multicultural make-up and saw beyond the romanticized Paris of guidebooks and tours. He loved to wander the more seedy sections, up and down the rue St-Denis, and look at the hookers.

"If you walk farther north on it past the tarts, you see the pink people," he informed me.

"The what?"

"They're pink. Some verging on puce, really."

"Puce," I stated, tone serious to match his.

"Yeah."

"Must remember to add 'puce' to some dinner conversation."

"They're heroine addicts," he said ignoring me. "And they turn pink."

"Or puce, when the case is severe."

He seemed to know about everything. He had a keen and observing eye that missed little, and the soul of a poet.

Ted loved people. He and Roland would stand together on the *place* talking about the world and its problems I think. A few times he even spent the night outside on the street with Roland. He knew far more about food than I and he taught me. We'd explore the Chinese markets, finding exotic fruit—litchi and longan, jack fruit and durian—and linger in the African markets absorbing the smells of spices and the cadences of the many languages. Most of all, Ted was a great dinner partner.

Together we would pour through the guidebooks selecting the perfect bistro to try out. In America, the word "bistro" has been corrupted. In France a bistro is a small restaurant usually with a handwritten blackboard or mimeographed menu and very traditional home-style cooking. It's the food I loved most: blood sausage and kidneys, *confit de canard* and *andouillette*. How, if not impossible, certainly improbable, to find this fare at a U.S. bistro (unless you're in New York.) Typical bistros have long zinc bars and white paper tablecloths. It's almost like dining in someone's home, although there are now some rather elegant and expensive ones.

A *brasserie*, on the other hand, tends to be bigger and more brightly lit. The word *brasserie* comes from the French word for brewery. The influence is Alsatian, so as well as beer, you will also find the white Riesling and Gewürztraminer, and plates of *choucroute* (sauerkraut) or platters of seafood. Everything else is a restaurant or a café, with the occasional exception of wine bar and tea salon.

Chapter 13

It was on a purely Parisian afternoon, when excitement hangs in the air like a great bird about to land, and everybody is out walking towards a *rendez-vous*, or else already there enjoying *un demi* or *un kir* or *un express* on the sidewalk of the Café Flore, that Ted and I strolled along the boulevard du Montparnasse on the way back from FNAC. The evenings were growing dark earlier, but it was around three in the afternoon so plenty of light still remained. Long shadows cast themselves along the streets as the sun moved west across Paris. People hustled by with bouquets of flowers or *baguettes* in hand. We passed the Select and then the Rotonde and I looked in at the table where I had last sat with Jason. An older gentleman with a hat and pipe sat at the table alone, reading his paper. I assumed he was happier than I had been, but in a passing glance how could one fathom an entire individual life?

I was hungry as we hadn't eaten since breakfast, and suddenly I turned to Ted and said, "Let's get oysters!"

"Brilliant idea. Where?" He loved them as much as I did. And it was an "R" month. You're allowed to eat oysters in the months that contain an "R." It's not that they will hurt you in the summer months as many people believe, only that the warm months are the spawning season and oysters can be thin and watery.

"Across the street, La Coupole. It's famous." La Coupole was synonymous with the words Art Deco and *brasserie*.

"We can't eat *out*. I thought you wanted to buy some to take back."

"I feel like eating out. Besides you've never been to the Coupole. It's a Parisian landmark. Each of the columns inside is painted by a different artist. Come on."

"But we can't," he protested.

"Why not?"

"The weasel!" he pointed to the pavement where "the weasel!" quite innocently stood.

"The weasel?" I started to laugh. "We'll take her in. She'll be fine."

"Kay, that dog is fanatical about food. I've never seen anything like it before and I'm sure I never will again. She'll be all over the table and lunging for everyone's plate. Be reasonable, and don't embarrass us both."

"She'll be fine. I know she will. Come on."

Ted, ever cool, was noticeably upset. I knew he was reluctant to follow me, but I guess his desire for oysters overcame him.

Even though I had seen dogs in restaurants before, I waited for the maitre d' to tell me my dog had to go. No one said a word and Lauren trailed along beside me on her leash, alert to the robust aromas of food. The great brasserie was still crowded and bustling from the lunch crowd, but thinning out a bit as people returned to work. We walked by soiled linen tablecloths, with half glasses of wine and water left standing, past gray heads bent forward in animated conversation, until we arrived at our table and I slipped in on the red banquette and put Lauren right beside me. Ted sat across from us.

"Hold her tight," he whispered.

"Don't worry." I had my arm around and in front of her so she couldn't climb on the table. The waiter took our order and then turned and asked if Lauren might like some water. Yes, thank you very much, she might. He came back with a bottle of Sancerre on ice and a chilled Badoit for us and placed before Lauren a sterling silver water bowl. Such was Lauren's introduction to French dining, and I knew from that moment that I'd done the right thing.

We ordered the oysters we both craved. I particularly liked the little, nutty-tasting Belons from Brittany, but increasingly more and more polluted water put these and other oysters in danger. When the waiter placed the big platter between us, I knew Ted would ignore the diminutive dishes of mayonnaise and *sauce Mignonette*, the shallots and vinegar, that many people put over the oyster before putting it on the generic pieces of rye toast and into their mouths. He would eat his oysters like I did, pure, with just a little juice from the lemon wedge.

"Okay, serious question sister dear," he looked at me. "Is it true they do what they're touted as doing?"

"Well, brother, I have never found it to be true myself, but what I understand is that they do in fact stimulate the appetite, something about the juices, more than any other food, activating the juices in your stomach. But no . . . not that appetite."

"My sentiments too. Escoffier called them, "the most palatable food known to man.'"

"And here's to Escoffier." We raised our glasses and drank the cool, acidic Sancerre that so well complemented the strangely delicious oysters. I raised the silver water bowl to Lauren to see if she would drink. Nope. No matter how thirsty she was, if food remained on the table, she wouldn't touch water. When she did drink, however, she consistently coughed back half of it, spewing water droplets everywhere. Amy said she was no different from everyone else in Virginia—she had a drinking problem.

"I would've loved to have been here in the twenties and thirties."

"The Coupole?" Ted asked, slurping down an oyster.

"Montparnasse. All of it. The Rotonde," I nodded across the street. "The Dôme, the Select. It all happened here, Kiki, Man Ray, the Americans. Before Montparnasse the intellectual center was Montmartre, then after the war it shifted from Montparnasse to St-Germain...Sartre and de Beauvoir, Café Flore and Deux Magots. Hemingway writes so well about the Brasserie Lipp."

"Yes. I've been to the Flore and Les Deux Magots, but never to eat at Lipp. For some reason it never seems accessible."

"It's wonderful. But, like the Flore and Deux Magots, you never sit on the terrace. The terrace is for tourists. Same with Flore. Inside at the Flore is good. Upstairs is best. Don't ask me why. Upstairs at Lipp is not. You might as well be dining in Siberia. Well, Siberia full of visiting Japanese and Americans.

"I wonder, do you think we're living through an era like Paris in the '20s and '30s but just don't know it?"

"I don't know, but I don't think so. It's not the same. I think we've gotten too far away…"

"But how do you know? I mean did they know it? Did they know they were making history? Who are the writers and philosophers today who could possibly compare?"

"There are people out there creating…many more actually. There's so much more of everything today…art, artists…than there was in their day."

"Maybe you can only know in retrospect, and then you can't really know because you're not around."

"Maybe."

Ted shifted in his chair.

"Can't believe how good she's being," He nodded at Lauren. I had removed my arm from around her neck, and she sat there beside me, upright and still. I broke off little bits of bread and fed her intermittently. Then I tried something new. I took a chunk of bread and placed it before her on the table while at the same time stating, "Stay." She transferred her gaze from the bread to my eyes and held my gaze. "Wait," I said. And she continued to watch me with the most intent stare. Then I said, "Okay." And she reached her head over on the table and snapped up the bread, gulped it down and turned back to me for more. Ted could not believe it.

"That's really amazing, considering her history. Wait till you tell Amy."

Ted stared at Lauren. I looked at Ted. He had the same dark eyes as I, but with a permanent twinkle (when he wasn't worrying about what I might try to do next with the weasel.) He caught my look and smiled at me. Then he shook his head, "She's something else, Kay." And that she was.

Later Ted read somewhere the word *chafouin*, which translates to "weasel-faced," and carries quite a negative connotation. He started calling Lauren *chafouin*, finding it terribly funny. I didn't find it funny, however, believing there was something altogether different in being called a weasel for the sound of it—the part Amy never could quite grasp—and being called one because you looked like one, especially when you were a dog.

Lauren was so well-behaved, I was proud, but also I was thrilled because it meant I could take her with me from now on, with or without company, whenever I ate out. Apart from outdoor cafés, La Coupole was her first restaurant, and it would be here that we'd return to celebrate her birthday each year. Since we never really knew her real birthday, I asked Amy to look on her calendar and tell me the date she discovered Lauren. She did. It was August the 8th. All my friends looked forward to Lauren's birthday celebration at the Coupole as if it were the big event of the year. I marveled at her devote following.

By the time we left La Coupole it was growing dark outside. The lights were coming on in apartment buildings and the yellow headlights crowded the great boulevards. The briny taste of seafood lingered in our mouths as the wine tingled in our bodies.

"October already, and I don't know where September went. Is that part of the human condition, our bizarre obsession with time? We're continually losing it, and I know few people who've ever found it again."

"She doesn't lose it," Ted nodded at Lauren. And I knew he was right. I knew that on some level, conscious or not, she accepted time, or its lack, in its truest essence, the present moment.

When a standard poodle fresh from the doggie salon walked by, Ted said, "Ornamental shrubbery." He always played a game of finding names for the people and dogs who passed us. I told him the big puffs and pom-poms on the poodles actually started in France around the time of Louis XIV, and were made to cushion and protect the joints when the dogs jumped into and swam in the water. The bows we see today were born of the original ribbons used to identify the dogs as they swam in competition. Most poodles in France, however, had the French clip without the pom-poms.

We walked home past the Closerie des Lilas and I thought of Lenin and Trotsky sipping vodkas at the bar. Hemingway, Pound, Joyce and the others. I turned to Ted.

"Okay, name something you can't live without."

"Passion," he said without hesitation.

"Passion...not love?"

"Passion for books, for music, for ideas, for the countryside, for the sea, for good food, for women...."

"I see."

"Okay, your turn."

"Lauren."

"How'd I know that was coming?" He sighed, then asked, "What's the highest compliment you can give someone?"

"To say that they make me laugh," I said with alacrity. "Guess that's what I always look for in someone."

"But we have Amy for that," he said and mimicked our sister: 'Are y'all laughing with me or *at* me? Oh, I don't care a lick if you do. Laugh all you want.'"

I laughed at his imitation. "Yeah, you're right, maybe she's spoiled us. What do you look for?"

"Um, let's see, intelligence, charm, kindness I should think. The older I get the more I understand the importance of kindness. When I was young, I wanted thrill and adventure, but now...."

"Ted," I said. "You *are* young." And we walked home in this fashion, quizzing each other about what was important and what it meant to be alive and young and walking the streets of Paris. I felt as if we were in a film and in a moment we'd turn fuzzy and blur out of sight. I was glad Ted was with me, and I was glad of the little dog who trotted along by my feet.

Chapter 14

The next day I had a meeting with several three-star chefs, and I knew the expedient thing to do would be to leave Lauren at home. Ted adamantly agreed, without sensing my apprehension. We walked by Roland, stiff, and just waking up.

"*Salut* Roland," we called. He grunted and when he asked us where we were going and why Lauren wasn't with us, I told him and pointed to the apartment. I jokingly asked if he wanted to come eat a good meal and he spit on the ground and waved a packet of rubbery grocery store ham in the air.

"What'd he say?" Ted asked.

"He said those chefs don't know how to cook, we're wasting our time." It was a known fact that Roland didn't eat. He drank his dinner instead.

We toured the kitchens of the Hôtel Crillon, after which Orwell had modeled the Parisian episodes in *Down and Out in Paris and London*. We ate a sumptuous lunch in the Jules Verne on the second floor of the Eiffel Tower, looking out across the extraordinary city. And all the while I kept thinking how I wished Lauren could have joined us there.

It was when we were walking home, and almost to the apartment door, that I heard in English the words, "and the dog was on the roof, and we said, "Save the dog!'" followed by a blur of conversation. Ted and I both stopped at the same time, turned and stared at each other, then turned to the proprietor of the voice. Two young, blond, American girls, students probably, sat on the rod-iron fence that surrounded the fountain.

"Excuse me," I ventured. "Did you say something about a dog?"

"Yeah," the one girl smiled. "There was a little dog running frantically back and forth up there!" She pointed to the awning of the café outside my window. "We kept yelling, '*Sauvez le chien, sauvez le chien!*' until the man from the *crêpe* stand," she pointed again, "jumped up there and put the dog back through the window. He closed it. But we thought the dog was gonna jump!" The girl was obviously proud of herself and her '*sauvez le chien.*' I was proud of her too. I thanked her, and Ted and I ran to the door, leaping up the stairs. The familiar click of the lock and the glass door being opened. Then through my own door. There she was, lying on her back, tail going thump, thump, thump on the floor.

We both looked to the window. I had left it cracked so the fresh air would come in, but Lauren had hopped up on an end table and gone out, looking for us. I had learned another lesson. Don't leave windows open.

I learned this lesson the hard way in the States as well. If, on a cool day, I took Lauren with me in the car to do errands, I could never leave her in a parking lot with the windows down, for she'd jump out and come find me. One day I was with Amy in her truck and we had Autumn, Bogie and Lauren with us in the front seat. We stopped in front of the frame shop where Amy had dropped off a lithograph. It was large so she'd wanted my help in carrying it. As the temperature crept up, I was afraid to leave the truck with the windows merely cracked for even minutes.

"Here," Amy said handing me a leash. "Leave them all the way down, just tie her up. She'll have the air and won't be able to go anywhere." I did and we went in, retrieved the giant print, and were walking out the shop door, when I saw her. There dangling from the leash, hind legs only inches from the asphalt, hung Lauren. I thought she was dead. I dropped the print, glass shattering over the sidewalk and ran the few steps, wordlessly. When I unclipped her, she collapsed on the ground stunned. I rubbed her neck where a mark remained and she looked up at me.

"That'll teach her," Amy walked up to us in her red cat-eyed sunglasses. Then she shook her head, "Kay, you've created a monster. Hey, and thanks for your help with the print."

I paid Amy for a new glass. I would have paid her for ten.

With Lauren in tow, Ted and I found the crêpe-stand man later that evening, and heard the rescue story again. He refused when I tried to reward him, but I persisted, for never would he understand my indebtedness and gratitude.

"It's okay," he said in French. "Really. Just come and buy my *crêpes*. And bring the little dog too."

Chapter 15

Ted left Paris vowing a return visit before I knew it. What I couldn't know then is that he would begin his own landscaping business, allowing less time for travel, and that in fact I would be returning to the States before his promised trip back.

I guess even the most planned-out lives can't prophesy what will happen to them in a year or five or ten, and that's the glory of it all, because we always have hope. Hope that there's a better life waiting or at least the steady continuation of the one we love. Hope is what keeps us going I'm certain. We only truly despair when we loose the capacity to hope. We're all alike in this way—the rich the poor, the white the black, the German the French. And when we can understand the fact that we're all in the same boat in the same ocean, we might stand a chance at peace, but I doubt we ever will. We, humans, have an anthropocentric view of things. I think and hope the animals will take over when we're gone. "Gone or destroyed in the name of progress," our collective tombstone will read. Animals have it figured out. I think they have more brains and certainly more heart. Meaning of life? Go ask your dog.

It was with and because of Lauren that I learned much about myself, and about others as well. Evidently all the things other people discovered years ago. I'm essentially a loner, but like every other human being from time immemorial, the mentally ill excepted, I needed other people, human contact. And, I wanted love. I wanted to be in that magical state of "coupledom." I thought I was easy-going and giving. I thought I was passionate and romantic. I worked well when coupled and I would've lived my whole life that way, had the choice always been left up to me. But why then, while in that wonderful couple, did my most meaningful moments happen alone? Lauren helped me solve this conundrum, for I was able to share fully with her what I couldn't always share with a lover. I realized that even in love, our most significant events are ultimately individual experiences.

"Yeah, sure, I know what you mean. Don't worry, you're not the lone ranger," Ted would say to me.

"Twit-brain, it's because you can be yourself with her," Amy was less tolerant of my revelations so late in life. "You don't lose your independence. That's what we humans are all searching for—to retain our separate selves, yet have a union with another. It's the human condition to want the impossible. If we got it—being human, an only moderately intelligent life form—we'd no longer long for it. We want to be accepted for who we are no matter what, and loved unconditionally. And who does this for us?" Pause. "Twit-brain, I'm talking to you."

"Yeah."

"Who does this for us? Our animals, that's who. And that's why you feel so close to Lauren. It's not that she's any great brain or anything. When you're talking all your philosophy crap and she's looking into your eyes and you think she's listening and loves you, all she's really thinking, if anything, is 'When is she going to feed me?'" And Amy was right. I did love Lauren for these reasons, and Lauren probably thought about food ninety percent of the time, and loved me because I fed her. But still I liked to think there was more to it than that. And as time went on I realized there was. Even Amy admitted that there *might* be.

I cannot ignore how fate insisted that I love this dog. We were two souls destined to be together. Two like-souls. She was to the canine race what I was to the human race. I can explain it no better than that. She was different. I was different. Together, we were alike. She stood beside me in all situations, and yet I knew she would not complete this life with me as a human mate might have. Yet, when I thought about it, it was Lauren who was my companion in life. I found in one small dog the love I'd been searching for throughout my life.

I remember a friend of mine once asked what my greatest or most heartfelt wish would be, could I have anything. And it surprised me as I'm sure it did him, when I said almost immediately,

"To be able to look up, for the rest of my life, and see her lying there." His question followed one of her bouts of pneumonia, so in retrospect, my response didn't surprise me at all. She was all I had on my mind.

But it was an impossible wish, and always to be so, and perhaps that is precisely why I so longed for it.

Maybe we love our dogs and cats more poignantly because we know theirs is a shorter lifetime. Why, when we start out the same age, does she have to grow old faster, overtaking me, and right before my eyes? Why their time on earth and with us must be so brief I don't know. Perhaps they are already good and pure and don't need to go through life a long while getting the lessons that we humans need. Maybe they are just here for the fun of it, the joy of life, a few good years.

A famous and well-respected film-star, who was also a friend of mine, lived for a while in Virginia with her equally famous movie-star and playwright husband. One day I held her in my arms and she cried and cried because her standard poodle had died. She told me she'd had the dog for eighteen years, "longer than any relationship."

So, there is this too. I admire the husbands and wives who manage to stay together all their lives, till death does them part. It has always been my elusive dream. A good marriage takes a lot of hard work. We all know that. But I think many couples do the hard work and still find they must part. It's only because we change, and we can only hope or try to change for the better. But change can sometimes mean different partners. Our animals are our one constant. This is what my movie-star friend felt, and the loss was tremendous.

But I digress. This is not her story, it's the story of a special dog.

Chapter 16

And so excited was I by my special dog and her excellent table manners, that I started dining out every night. Often it was to review a restaurant, but even when I had no work to do, I went out to eat. Lauren loved it.

When we were feeling lazy, we'd just stroll down the rue Mouffetard and take a right on a little pedestrian street, the rue du Pot-de-Fer. Restaurants lined this street, none of them very good, but the throngs of tourists sitting down didn't seem to mind. My neighborhood attracted the tourists in droves, those seeking the "real" Latin quarter, in the same way they flocked to St-Germain, pursuing quintessential Paris. They found the *quartier* Mouffetard irresistibly quaint. Because of them, the quarter was becoming a bit less quaint. It was a shame, but I knew of no spot, picturesque and charming, unless remote and inaccessible, that this fate did not befall, the French Rivièra exemplifying the phenomenon at its most horrific.

There were a few southwestern restaurants—French southwestern, not American—serving the fare for which I yearned poignantly when in the States. The multitude of American southwestern and Tex-Mex restaurants that had popped up recently appeared to be a craze that might become permanent. They would insinuate themselves into the structure of French cuisine so much so that the new generation of students and writers and artists "who changed their sky, but not their souls, as they flew across the sea," would believe that the Mustang Café had co-existed down the road from Le Dôme for an eternity. Perhaps in a way it had.

In my neighborhood in about a 200-yard radius I could count more than ten different cuisines: Russian, Mexican, Créole, Spanish, Greek, North-African, Italian, Chinese, Vietnamese, Thai, Japanese, Jura-Savoie, Sud-Ouest, Brêton, and of course classical French. The fast-food joints were ousting many of the sit-down restaurants, but they were in a class of their own.

My favorite restaurant, however, on the pedestrian street was a "quaint" little spot called Chez Robert with handwriting on the walls, literally. Pierre Charles Le Metayer, a friend and renowned blood-stock agent, had taken me there once, for as he explained he used to frequent it when he was a student in the quarter. That was many years ago. So maybe I liked Chez Robert for its disregard of the migrant restaurants that came and went, for its tradition and staying power. The proprietress had short blond hair and blue eyes like a Normande and was always pleased to see me, but overjoyed to see Lauren. We usually ate at an outside table, side by side, and received a legion of attention from the street-walkers.

Frequently I would have the same meal, snails to start, followed by a *frisée* salad with poached egg, followed by *confit de canard*, the delicious crispy duck preserved in its own fat, with garlic potatoes. A pitcher of house red, and a bottle of Badoît. Cheese and dessert if space permitted, and always an *express* to finish things off. Lauren feasted on bread and bites of duck and potato. Afterwards, we would walk home slowly, the back way over the rue Tournefort, fat and happy, pleased to be thinking about sleep as the rest of Paris geared up for the night.

Paris is a beautiful city at night. Speeding along the Seine in a taxi, unable to remove my eyes from the Eiffel Tower lit up at its most omnipotent, or the illuminated Conciergerie, where Marie-Antionette was imprisoned—I sometimes thought that there was no other city to touch this one at night.

On this particular evening, however, I was not feeling lazy and longed for the real sense of Paris, the bowels of the city or maybe the heart of the city. I needed to get out of my own neighborhood, for it was beginning to feel too crowded. I wanted to share a new experience with my dog. We took the métro to Jourdain on the border of the nine-teenth and twentieth *arrondissements*, another world from where I lived. These were traditionally working-class or very ethnic sections of Paris, although the nineteenth was becoming trendy after the introduction of La Vilette. Many first-timers to Paris missed these areas, except perhaps to give a cursory glance to the tombs of Chopin, Colette, Piaf, Delacroix,

Abélard and Héloïse, Simone Signoret, Yves Montand, and Jim Morrison in the cemetery of Louis the XIV's confessor, Père Lachaise. But here you could find the pulse of Paris, everyday life as it had existed for decades and beautiful nineteenth-century buildings. I stepped back into a Zola novel every time I walked these streets. Lauren trotted along beside me, sniffing for food. But the crumbs here were the same as in the fifth *arrondissement*, and neither the ethnicity nor the architecture impressed her sensibility. Thinking of Ted, I had studied the Gault Mihault guide and Patricia Wells before setting out to find just the right restaurant, for I liked to explore an area with a destination in mind.

We were high up in the section of Paris called Belleville, a hilly, villagey area that was absorbed into the city during the nineteenth century. We walked south from the church of St-Jean-Baptiste-de-Belleville, and down the rue des Envierges to stand and gaze out over the Parc de Belleville and the immensity of Paris sprawling to the south and west beyond. The evening air was soft and I wore only a light jacket. I picked Lauren up so she could see the view, then did what I always did. I kissed her mouth, just beneath her nose, where the whiskers brushed forward like a catfish and the little hairs around her mouth tickled, but felt good. I never knew another dog with a more perfect "kissing spot" as Amy called it. As the years went by that spot became worn away, by all my kissing I guess. She rarely kissed me back, but I knew she loved me, for I read it in her eyes and saw it in her actions. She rarely lapped with her tongue the way some dogs did to show happiness. Nor, for that matter, did she ever play much with the stuffed toys I saw other dogs toss up in the air and shake violently in trying to snap at the neck. At first I thought she disdained the toys. But then I realized she probably figured, what's the use of killing it if you can't eat it afterwards?

We turned back from the Parc de Belleville and headed for a restaurant that had caught my eye in passing, Le Zephyr. It still had tables outside so I pulled out two chairs side by side, placed Lauren in one while I slide into the other, and sat beneath the pruned bows of the plane trees.

She sat upright as I ordered, becoming increasingly more attentive when the food was placed before us. She watched as I ate a perfectly cooked plate of *rougets*, the red mullet found along the Mediterranean coast. Her eyes never wavered as they followed my fork along its predictable course. I ate a bite, then offered her one. She ate off my fork with dignity. I put one on the table and said, "Stay," and she turned her gaze to me and waited until the magic word, "Okay" to politely grab it, and swallow in one gulp.

We sat together eating then pausing, talking then observing, for what seemed a long time. A feeble man walked by planting his cane and his feet carefully, while his smiling face belied any uncertainty, and I thought, not for the first time, that it's all in one's regard. The air got colder, yet never chilled us. The leaves from the plane trees blew on the sidewalk. Finally after a chocolate concoction of dessert, of which Lauren did not partake, we left and headed south towards the quarter of Ménilmontant. I took back streets that were deserted except for the shadows and an occasional hum of voices from behind closed doors. Anti-Le Pen graffiti graced several derelict facades. When we were opposite the cemetery of Père Lachaise, I glanced over beyond the high wall, thinking momentarily of Molière's play and decided it was time to hop on a métro.

Lauren was exceptionally trusting. You hear praised those singular souls who are tolerant to the intolerant. I was not such, quickly losing patience with those whose opinions offended me, and yet, paradoxically, my dog was.

She stepped up onto the métro, never fearfully balking at the looming gap or the noise. She also marched right up the moving escalator with its funny groves the first time I ever asked her to, even though I could read apprehension in her eyes. Tonight she settled into my lap, with her head resting on my arm, and slept on the near empty métro as it rattled from side to side. By the time we crawled up the steps and I pulled out the bed we were both pooped.

I put Lauren on the side of the bed where she always slept, her brown head creating a small dent in the pillow. I climbed in beside her and stroked her ears. She was out. She always slept most soundly after eating out. She started to snore lightly and I watched her, my mind marveling at this little stray who'd nearly died and who now lay fast asleep in a bed with the covers pulled up to her shoulders; who dined better than most people, in the best restaurants in that most famous of all cities, Paris. This was a rags to riches story if ever I'd seen one. It was also, I would come to realize later, a true labor of love. I stroked her head resting on its own pillow, remembering the perfect evening. But can such moments of peace and happiness endure?

Lauren's Story

Chapter 17

When I woke my hand was still on her head and she'd hardly moved. I stepped out of bed.

"Come on Lauren."

She was full of sleep. I said her name and her tail moved, flap, flap, flap. Who designed these mechanisms? We smile, they wag their tags. Sometimes she was lazy and loved to sleep in. I had to rouse her to get her up, but always the call for breakfast would do it.

"Lauren. Let's eat."

I heard a knocking sound and went to open the door, but it was Lauren's tail slapping against the table legs.

I fed her breakfast, complete with drugs, then poured myself a bowl of Grapenuts, sent to me from my mother in the States, and made a strong cup of coffee with the *cafétière*. Lauren finished her own food in twenty seconds and hopped up on the opposite chair at the kitchen table.

"Lauren I'm not going to feed you again. You just ate."

She stared at me with pricked ears, so I turned my gaze to the people milling about on the square. I waved to Roland who had given me two dozen fresh eggs a couple days ago and then asked if I needed any money, pulling out a wad of bills. He was the only bum I knew who had more money than I did.

"Lauren, Jimmy's out there."

She didn't even turn her head.

"Okay, okay." I offered her a spoonful of Grapenuts and watched as she lapped it up, spilling milk all over the table. We did this every morning and every morning she never failed to retain a little milk mustache, or beard, on her chin whiskers. Since she never wiped it off, I did.

After breakfast Lauren raced out the door to play with Jimmy, on whom she'd developed quite a crush, then we set out via the bus

79

Lauren, six weeks out of intensive care and still skinny. This was the photograph Amy sent to me in Paris.

Amy and her dogs. Apache and Bogie are in front on the left. Little Autumn is directly in front.

Growing attached to each other at
Amy's house.

Lauren spoke to my soul. She was accepting, never complained, lived
each day in the present, and when I did things to her she didn't like, she chose
forgiveness over revenge.

I can see her eyes, fixed with abiding hope upon the croissant, as if it might leave the plate on which it lay.

Café hopping with Ted and Texas friend Judy along the fashionable avenue Victor Hugo.

Lauren and Roland at
the café below my
apartment.

Lauren in the Paris apartment.

Lauren decided to stride up to every restaurant and proceed in through the door.

I would talk to her and she'd look into my eyes, never doubting a word I said.

Lauren, me, the fountain and the place de la Contrescarpe, taken from my kitchen window.

At the gates of the Palais Royal.

Playing with Jimmy, oblivious to the fact that her long leash had become a hazard to pedestrians walking by.

In the Luxembourg Gardens. It was here that we were our happiest.

Road kill imitation.

Lauren is diagnosed with cancer.

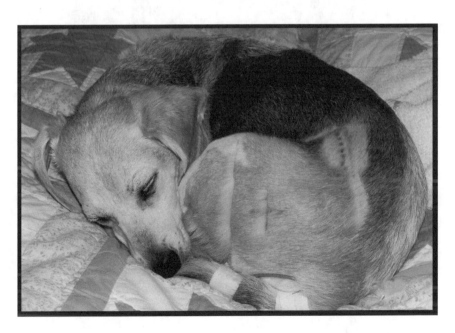

Lauren with funny marks from radiation and the catheter taped to her tail.

Lauren, a year and a half after being diagnosed with cancer.

for the luscious and residential seventeenth *arrondissement*. As a child I had hurt my neck in a skiing accident, and consequently suffered back pain ever since. I had an appointment with an old friend and osteopath, Giles de Gasté.

I herded Lauren into the tiny elevator and pushed the sixth floor. When Giles answered the door we embraced warmly cheek to cheek. He led me into a room that might have been the library of a prominent diplomat. The walls were lined with leather-bound books while Aubusson and Beauvais carpets covered the floor. It was a doctor's office, but no white, sterile walls or paper covering were visible, and, of course, dogs were permitted. I found it ironic that about the only building in Paris Lauren was never allowed to enter was the American Consulate.

Giles and I caught up on what we and mutual friends had done over the past year. He told me he'd very recently left his wife; I said nothing about my broken romance, for there was nothing to say.

Giles was handsome, an attractiveness shaped by intelligence. European men and women have a different look than do our American counterparts. In the U.S. there's the all-American or Californian kind of looks. Blonde hair, blue eyes, obligatory tan. But it could feel and even look superficial, even if it wasn't. A European beauty is more encompassing: it's imperfect, yet there is a poise, a grace, and a charm as much as a physical beauty, and it goes deeper than skin. Once you recognize it, it's unmistakable. Nureyev had it. So too did Marcello Mastroianni.

I told Giles the trouble I'd been having with my neck and back, for I'd been writing at my desk a lot, and he massaged and manipulated my shoulders. Lauren lay perfectly still with her head resting on her front paws observing the two of us the entire time. Giles dutifully admired her, and upon leaving we made a date to have dinner.

Leaving the rue Faraday I knew exactly where we were going for a mid-morning snack: the wonderful market on the rue Poncelet. There in the hours just before lunch the market was in full swing. I bought a barquette of *fraises de bois*, the tiny wild strawberries that are so flavorful and two beautifully baked warm croissants. The street was crowded and all of a sudden I heard a croak of dismay, "*Oh! Mademioselle, regard!*" I did regard and I saw that Lauren had taken a bite out of a lady's *baguette*. The woman had been holding the bread perilously low. In consternation

I began to offer sincere apologies, but to my amazement, her old face twisted into the warmest and most gracious of smiles and she began to chuckle. She explained to me that she had two *petite caniches*, (poodles) and said what a dear Lauren was, she didn't mind a bite out of her bread. *"C'est le même que j'achete tous les jours. Il sera là demain, aussi."* I smiled in gratitude. The Parisians weren't as bad as everyone said. I grabbed a bottle of Volvic and with goodies in hand we headed to the Parc Monceau.

Elegant. The Parc Monceau is elegant—or maybe it merely attracts an elegant crowd. We walked slowly around the park, while school girls in dark blue uniforms ran and screeched excitedly. I found the apartments on the southern side some of the most beautiful in Paris. One day, I thought, I might like to try living there. It never hurt to fantasize. Louis Carmontelle sure had. In the eighteenth century he designed the park Monceau to be a magical place, complete with Roman temple, pyramid, pagoda and feudal ruins. Some remnants and ruins still remained. After walking around I found an empty bench on one end and we sat side by side to eat our snack, the sunlight falling upon us and making shadows through the trees like a Pissaro painting.

We left the park and walked down the boulevard Malesherbes past the church of St-Augustine with its commanding dome, the brown leaves from the plane trees whirling around our feet on the sidewalk. I was a fast walker, but walking with Lauren was invariably a slow process since she investigated each tree and the sides of every building. Yet she taught me to slow down and to stop and look around me, not only toward the splendid architecture of Paris, but also to something that was invisible to the eye and could only be felt, the pulse of life, both present and past.

When we got to the church of the Madeleine with its fifty-two Corinthian columns, I debated whether to walk on to the Opéra and hop on the métro, a direct line home, or to keep walking, for while rain clouds hovered, it was still a perfect day. On we went, down the rue Royale en route to what many consider the world's most beautiful square, the place de la Concorde. Sometimes in Paris it was best to look with new eyes, those of the high-school students over for the first time, the ones who didn't read their history prior and who forgot their guidebooks. History was why I loved the city. But history could overwhelm. Every cobblestone told a story—gory, glorious or notorious. The place de la Concorde, which had seen the beheading of Louis XVI, Marie-Antoinette and Madame du Barry, so etched in historians' minds, so familiar to the rest of us, ceased to shock. But other sights of massacre, more recently blood-stained, like the bullet hole through the window of Joe Goldenberg's on the rue des Rosiers, could make me feel the precariousness of life.

Before reaching the classical square, I took a right on the rue du Faubourg St-Honoré. We passed Gucci and Lanvin, and walked in through the doors of Hermès. Lauren's worn-out pads welcomed the soft carpet of the great store. I needed a few birthday presents and I knew I could find picture frames or desk-top ornaments apposite to the occasion that wouldn't cost a fortune. As I enquired about items, Lauren lay down, her muzzle resting between her two front paws, her hind legs stretched out behind her. Then she rolled over on her back and started a round of the squirmies. In an instant, all the BCBGs flocked around, cooing over my dog. By now BCBG, or *bon chic, bon genre* was on the map of international lingo along with yuppie and Sloane Ranger. But less well-known was CPFH or *collier perle, foulard Hermès* (pearl necklace, Hermès scarf). And all the CPFHs and BCBGs were right there, the real thing in the flesh, or in Céline tasseled loafers, fawning over Lauren. We left in a hurry.

We walked along under the arcaded rue de Rivoli for a bit before crossing over into the Tuileries. I knew dogs were prohibited in these gardens, but I figured we'd take our chances. When given the chance I always preferred to walk through a garden. Lauren sniffed the trees and I studied the sculpture. Tourists marched earnestly towards the Arc du Carroussel and beyond it the centuries-old Louvre, with its brand new pyramid. I wondered how they got along. From the looks of it, quite well. I'd witnessed so many of Mitterand's *grands projets* in the making that had now become integral and time-worn emblems of Paris. I smile when I think that I'll get to say to all the young twenty-first-century whipper-snappers after me that, "I lived in Paris at the turn of the century. I knew it before the Pyramide du Louvre, the Arche de la Defense, or La Villette." Just as those before me at the turning of a different century knew it before that most Parisian of all landmarks, the

Eiffel Tower. It gave perspective.

We crossed the Pont du Carrousel just as rain clouds, swollen and seeking moisture's egress, began to drip the first light droplets of water onto us. Up the rue Bonaparte as the sky above turned dark. Walkers picked up their pace, and umbrellas popped out. Lauren and I had none. Over the rue Visconti and up the rue de Seine to glance in La Palette (wave to Karl Lagerfeld, who doesn't wave back), but the place was packed and I could see no free tables. We walked back toward St-Germain-des-Prés on the rue Jacob and by this time the rain was coming down hard. Lauren was walking too slowly and her stomach was filthy and drenched from the splash. She was unhappy, so I scooped her up, and jogged along with her in my arms, which she found decidedly better.

I ran across the boulevard St-Germain dodging cars and up the rue des Canettes, named for those ducklings. We headed for the Café de la Mairie on the place St-Sulpice. There we ducked inside and found a table with only one seat, so I held the bedraggled beagle on my lap. (Smile at Bernard-Henri Lévy and Elisabeth Badinter, who don't smile back.)

"*Mademoiselle.*"

"*Un café, s'il vous plaît.*"

"*Et bonjour le chien. Tout mouillé, oh.*" She was adored wherever we went and the waiter came back with a dish towel and wiped her head and back dry. Within minutes the clouds had rolled back and the sun slipped out creating a world that glistened with freshness, the contrast always sharp after a shower. I paid for the coffee and set Lauren on the ground to try her own legs again. I looked up to St-Sulpice on my left, a church I have never found aesthetically beautiful, but one of my favorites nevertheless—perhaps it's the location. The first time I went in it while with Lauren, I dutifully tied her outside. But when sitting down, I could hear her rare mournful cry, I jumped up and carried her inside. She'd been in many times since, usually carried in my arms as propriety behooved. We didn't stop to go in this time, but headed up the wonderful little rue Férou to the Luxembourg gardens. Hemingway lived on this street too and I envy him that.

WE CROSS THE rue de Vaugirard and go in the exit near the Orange-rie, this section forbidden to dogs. I am not worried. At least we are walking toward the dog area, not away from it as so often we are, and we stroll slowly soaking up the greenery and diffident sunbeams. We walk right around by the base of the palace and past all the guards, but they are not the ones patrolling the grounds; they are only concerned with protecting the palace itself.

The little café of the Luxembourg sits near the Medici fountain in the shade of the trees. Some of the leaves have already fallen, but many remain. I'm starving and, except for a brief stint in my arms and the respite at the Café de la Mairie, Lauren's short legs have been walking most of the day.

There are plenty of tables and chairs outside. I wipe two off and Lauren hops up on her own chair and sits beside me patiently. She understands what this means. I know it will take a long time to be served. It always does. And when we are, the little man will try to push the *Baba au Rhum* on me. He always does. But I know I want the heaping plate of lentils and a *citron pressé*. And however mediocre the food, the ambience makes up for it. So does the company. Her eyes stare into mine and I say, "Lauren I'm going to feed you, you just have to wait." Behind us the bells of St-Sulpice begin to chime.

A TRANSCENDANT tranquility engulfed me as I sat in the shadows of the chestnuts at the outside table with Lauren beside me. The fountain splashed in the background and I knew that happiness was not one tangible concept to be enjoyed indeterminately, but something ephemeral existing in isolated moments.

One afternoon in the Luxembourg I brought my camera, took off my tinted sunglasses and placed them before the lens. An amateur's attempt, but the photos came out surprisingly well and the slight aure-ate glow makes them appear from a previous time. One picture I took that day has remained propped up on my desk. In it Lauren sniffs in the shadow of a tree in the far right-hand corner of the foreground. The light shines down and dapples the earth where people stroll casu-ally or sit on the green chairs under a canopy of branches and leaves. In the background the light is so bright it becomes blurry and white, but you can make out the cement railing and the flower pots filled and overflowing. One moment recorded, frozen in time. Strangers, only the dog I know. I often gaze at that picture and it takes me there in a way that nothing else can.

And on those days I go there with her.

In no hurry to leave, we stayed there together a long time. But finally I knew I had work to finish at my desk. The earlier rain had turned the afternoon cool, and we walked up the rue Soufflot ready to be home. Lauren, nose ever to the ground, at once leaped back crying out. I went over to her to investigate the still burning cigarette butt she'd tried to eat, but it wasn't that this time. She'd shocked her nose on a wet wire from a café light fixture. She looked up at me dejectedly and I told her it wasn't her fault, but that maybe in the future she shouldn't attempt to eat wires.

I wrote a lengthy film review that evening at my desk. The film had starred Daniel Auteuil and I'd thought it excellent. Yet my article was poor. I kept trying, but couldn't get it right. I felt the despondency I always did when I didn't write well, the same as the elation I felt when I did. I looked up from the mess I'd scrawled, and crossed out a dozen times, and saw Lauren rolling on her back, doing "the squirmies" on the sofa. My mood lifted, my mouth smiled and my heart jumped.

Chapter 18

Together we walked every cobblestone of Paris. From Montmartre to the Butte aux Cailles, the Butte Chaumont to the parc Montsouris. The gardens of the Palais Royal, the Champs de Mars, and Lauren's favorite, the rose garden in the Bagatelle.

I took her inside La Sainte Chapelle, where the guard informed me she's one of few dogs to have gone in, gone upstairs and beheld those awe-inspiring, chill-inducing, wondrous stained-glass windows.

We watched the seasons come and go. Spring in any place is pretty amazing. In Paris it's poignant. It's what you've been waiting for all winter, when the first of the café tables appears outside on the sidewalk, the flowers start blooming everywhere you turn your glance and a breeze of anticipation floats through the air. I loved the cool morning air coming through the open windows. It offered such expectancy. And as the sun rose, the day would warm up, but then evening would return to me again the cool breeze I knew only to belong to spring, to my childhood of cut green grass, as cool as nightfall.

This year to celebrate the arrival of spring I took Lauren to one of the little lakes in the Bois de Boulogne. We rented a canoe. I took the stern and she took the bow and off we paddled. How ironic, I'd always wanted to do this with a lover, for I thought it so romantic. Here I was instead with my dog.

"Lauren get your head *out* of the picnic bag and look around."

She knew I had to keep paddling so she kept right on.

"I hope you can swim, weasel." Still she ignored me. I paddled over to the island and pulled the canoe up onto the verdant banks. I spread out a blanket and put the food on top.

"What makes you think you deserve anything at all? I didn't see you rowing." She gave me her snobby look and lay down, keeping her eyes on the bag of food. Then I threw it back into the canoe so she'd walk around a little first. I wasn't ready to eat yet.

The air currents were warm and cool, like those areas in a lake, and they wafted over us deliciously signaling the changing of the seasons. Transition time. The new leaves were that special green that only lasts a short time and were still small and folded down like sleeping bats. In a few weeks they'd be large and luscious, a deeper green. But now the promise of spring was yet in the air.

I let Lauren out to the end of her lease and she snorkeled around in the grass, nose to the ground, then sat rudely staring at a family a ways off having their picnic lunch. I plucked one of those ubiquitous weeds—the kind we used to make "violins" out of when we were kids—and tried to make the strings, but it broke. I took out a book of verse and lay back against a tree to enjoy the sweetness of this particular day in my life.

Minutes strung together turned into an hour. When my stomach spoke I sat back up.

"Lauren, come on." No response whatsoever. She was at the end of her long leash, staring at a paper bag out of reach. I knew the only way to get her attention was to retrieve my own food bag. The crinkling sound would do it.

I pulled out a hunk of Cantal cheese, then some sliced *pain Poilâne*. She smelled it. Head snapped around, ears pricked, and she shuffled over in my direction and sat very still watching me, waiting for what she knew she'd receive.

I poured water in a cup for us both. I drank, she would not. I tore off pieces of the bread, making her do her trick of waiting for a moment before she ate. I read Ronsard to her, but she had no interest in poetry and I put it aside. Deciding the cheese was too fatty for her, but not for me, I ate it all and pretended that our picnic consisted only of bread and peaches. I bit into an almost ripe *pêche blanche*, my favorite, then offered it to Lauren. She took a bite avoiding the pit, looked pleased with herself and waited for more. I took a bite; she took a bite. Then she became over-zealous and tried to chomp the whole peach, pit and all.

"Greed gets you nowhere fast, Lauren. Try again."

She took a dainty bite this time and chewed it up.

A glance at my watch told me it was time to turn in the canoe. We would have to hurry. We returned the wooden boat in time, walked for quite a while then took the number 82 bus home. While the Paris métro system is safe and the most efficient one I know, if I couldn't walk to a place, I'd take the bus, and only as a last resort, the métro. There was certainly a difference in the people who rode the bus and those who took the métro. Usually older, more affluent ladies rode the bus. When I was a student, I'd hop on any bus and go anywhere, then hop off and get on another. Hop off and walk home from who knows where. It was a great way to see the city. With a few outstanding exceptions the métro is all underground.

Years later it's funny what you remember. We were on the number 63 bus once, which runs along the rue des Ecoles in my neighborhood, and then on through the faubourg St-Germain in the sixth and stately seventh, past the National Assembly and the Invalides, along the Seine. I sat in the back, my head turning this way to look towards the Palais Bourbon, then that way towards the Place de la Concorde and the gilded bridge of Alexandre III. Lauren was sitting on the seat next to me, when a scruffy-looking older man stumbled on, the kind you'd expect to see on the métro, not the bus. He sat down and began talking to the NAP (Neuilly, Autieul, Passy) ladies around him as well as to me. Silence. No one even looked up. He could've been a leper the way the involuntary movements rippled from one woman to the next, and the rigid non-glances, an unspoken language unto themselves, slithered among the old staid faces. More harmful to the soul than an actual physical blow is an emotional shunning. At least the physical blow carries human contact. I realized something was wrong with him, that he was simple-minded or slow, and I nodded and smiled, but, between the French and his slur, I couldn't for the life of me understand a word he spoke. Then he directed all his attention toward Lauren and he babbled and smiled, babbled and drooled. Through all the babbling the only thing I could make out was that he "had had a dog, that looked like Lauren, ate green beans and lived to be seventeen." Presently, he became silent, his eyes tearing up the way some old people's do. I looked over and saw that Lauren's head was resting on his knee. He stroked the top of her head. As I said, it's odd what we remember. I've often thought about that man with the seventeen year-old dog who ate green beans. If he has no relatives, at least there is one person who thinks of him.

97

I like animals because they are blind to our prejudices. Lauren gave the simple, old man the love and physical contact he probably hadn't had in who knows how long. For one moment she gave him love and acceptance and I think his tears were because of her and overwhelming emotion, not failing tear ducts. How hard it is to accept people as they are and not judge. Amy was the only human I knew who was truly blind in this respect. She really didn't *see* differences. If she caught me judging a person, she admonished me, "Don't judge, Kay, till you've walked in the other guy's shoes. 'Course it helps if he has good taste in shoes."

Once again I looked to Lauren. She didn't judge. If she could reason, she would divide the world into those who gave her food and those who did not.

During her years in Paris, Lauren went to some rather remarkable places: parties at the Crillon and the Invalides, the humidor in Paris' most venerable cigar shop. Once I smuggled her into the Prix de l'Arc du Triomphe at Longchamp, the most prestigious horse race in France. When I took her out of the zipped bag, a gloved and hatted woman came running over, something rattling forth from her mouth and balanced a hat (a real hat, a Stephen Jones hat, probably a $400 hat—not a party hat) on Lauren's small head. My friend Marc translated the woman's outburst to, "*Oh là*, but she must wear a hat or she's not proper." The woman was laughing. I was stunned to find a joke amongst the stiff formality of the racing world. Lauren defused some of the stuffiness surrounding this particular social event. The French will do anything for a dog. I have a picture of Lauren in that hat—but when she acted humiliated, I took it off as soon as the lady left. I never knew whose hat it was.

Lauren later traveled to Los Angeles, which she didn't much like, Washington and New York. She rode beside me down the Promenade des Anglais as I drove a 1948 Talbot Lago, and she rode in a '55 Lancia (Pinin Farina) along the Grande Corniche. Few men can boast to that; still fewer dogs.

She also met some rather remarkable people, such as the Agha Kahn, the Prince and late Princess of Wales and a multitude of movie stars, including, once in Paris, her namesake, Lauren Bacall. Yet she never discriminated, or esteemed those with titles or money above those who had not.

One of Lauren's biggest fans was a great patron of the arts as well as, in her youth, an avid stag hunter. The Comtesse de Fougereaux lived at number 67, quai Branly with the Eiffel Tower in her backyard. We were frequently invited to be her dinner guests and this allowed us to meet all kinds of interesting people. It was always a magical experience as we stood or sat on her ground floor terrace, sipping champagne or *kir royals*, flowering bushes, unreconizable to me, cascading over the stone railing and the Tour Eiffel—so close you felt you could just touch it—illuminated like a backdrop. Then we'd have dinner and conversation, with the emphasis on the latter, in a dining room, all Regency and Louis XV, real, not reproduction.

The first time I ever showed up with Lauren, invited by a friend of mine who also knew the countess, the countess fell in love with my dog at first glance.

"What soulful eyes she has." She stroked Lauren, turning all her attention to her, and ignoring a question from a guest behind her back. "Her ears are quite the softest I've felt. What do you do to them?"

I laughed. But it wasn't a joke and she continued,

"My father had one very similar in Normandy. Has she seen Normandy?"

"No."

"Then you must take her. I think she'd like it."

"Okay."

"You absolutely must."

"I'll take her."

Then to Lauren she said, "Perhaps you're related to *Tambour*." I didn't tell the countess Lauren wasn't a French beagle.

When we sat down to eat, I told Lauren to "Stay" in the drawing room.

"Oh no, no. She will dine with us," declared the countess, leaving not an inch of room for protest. "Here. This chair seems made for her." And she pulled up a beautiful, but very small chair, no doubt dating from the seventeenth-century when people were smaller. I was doing my best not to act stunned. The countess then looked at me and said, "From now on that will be Lauren's chair."

On one typical evening Lauren sat in her chair throughout the entire nine-course dinner, quite alert unlike one guest who'd imbibed too much Bordeaux and began to emit noises through his mouth and nose when his chin slumped to his chest. When we retired to the salon Lauren still remained sitting erect in her chair listening to the conversation and watching each person as he or she spoke. When the countess was asked what she thought about the recent happenings in Algeria, hundreds having been gruesomely slaughtered, she replied, "I found it a bit agitating." I knew she was anything but cold and insensitive as many said of her, and that her façade was just that, a façade, hiding something deeper. She had a beautiful sense of humor, you just had to catch it.

I sat beside my dog and wondered what she was thinking on these occasions. I'm sure she had her own ideas on the situation in Algeria or in the Middle East that far surpassed those being expressed. No, actually I suspect her mind still thought about the giant *gigot* we'd eaten and hoped and believed there would be more to come. Lauren had a one-track mind. Of that I am almost sure.

Chapter 19

I'd been writing reviews religiously for *The Poop on Paris* since acquiring the job. When I told people about the work I did, it always sounded glamorous, but like all jobs, it could in fact be tedious. I decided I could afford a week's holiday, and that a change of pace and scenery might actually improve my work. I shuffled together some things and shoved them in a bag. Lauren and I were going to Normandy. I had promised the countess, hadn't I? I also wanted to show Lauren the Norman coast. Loving oysters so much, I had taken her to Brittany—-from St-Malo on the northern coast, to the Point du Raz in the west, and Quiberon on the south, then tasting the famous oysters of Locmariaquer. I think a part of me came from there, for I felt drawn to the wildness, a ruggedness not unlike the coast of Maine or Nova Scotia. And yet I also loved the Mediterranean mentality and landscape; perhaps I loved the Mediterranean most of all, and therefore Lauren had been to Provence and the French Rivièra an untold number of times. She'd even gone to Italy. From an inauspicious start in the back woods of Virginia, she had become a cosmopolitan dog.

Since we had always headed south in search of sun, now we'd head northwest toward the bucolic Norman countryside. I had a conscious feeling that I wanted to share everything I held important in my soul with the one creature I knew would instinctively understand. If she didn't understand in the literal or historical way that I did, I knew she would understand on a visceral level. We communicated by our presences. There was also, this time, another feeling.

When we got on the train for Caen at the Gard de Nord, I kept Lauren in her bag until the controller had come through, for, like aboard the airplane, I was to have bought her a ticket. I knew she wouldn't bark, but I was afraid she might snore so loudly we'd be caught.

I loved trains, much preferring them to planes. I put my face to the glass as we pulled out. As the train gathered speed, apartments and houses—-the suburbs of Paris—-flashed by. Then the houses became fewer, and expanses of green, with *bocages* took over. Hayfields, poplars, grazing Charolais, stone farmhouses, stone churches. We pulled into several small, sparsely populated towns, slowing down and finally grumbling to a stop. A handful of people stood waiting on the quai, uncertainly. Doors opened and closed. When I saw the black and white spotted *vache Normande* standing beneath an apple tree, I knew we were in Normandy. Just like the postcards. The roofs were all gray slate with a sky to match, just as in the south they are red tile next to a sky, that new eggshell blue. The air had a wet, salty feel to it even though the sea was still some miles away. Finally people stood, reached for luggage in the racks above and lurched down the aisle ways toward openings. The train slowed and the outskirts of Caen became visible in their ugliness, most of the city having been blown away during the Second World War.

Lauren sprang to life in the Hertz office, rolling on her back and snapping in the air for me or someone to play with her. I filled out and signed the papers as Lauren did the twist by my feet, then we jumped in a tiny Renault and were off. Lauren loved riding in cars, and went right to sleep—I guess the movement, or my proximity, gave her comfort.

Even though Caen is the capital of Normandy, I had little desire to stay in there, and drove west on the N13 taking Lauren first to Bayeux. When we parked and walked along a tree-shaded street, I realized how happy I was to be away from that larger city, Paris. Closer to the sea, I would realize this all the more. It's hard to get lost in Bayeux, or any French town for that matter, for there is always the spire of the cathedral, or perhaps the bell-tower of a Romanesque church, to locate you. In this case it was the Cathérale de Notre Dame. Our Lady worked over time for brief period in history, several centuries. I faithfully admired the exterior, particularly the portal on the south side of the transept, where the tympanum depicts the assassination of the English Archbishop of Canterbury Thomas Becket, on the orders of Henry II. I wasn't a huge fan of gothic architecture, preferring instead the simplicity of Romanesque, but this cathedral, like many, combined the two. The Normand style of architecture, created by the Benedictine monks, later spread to England and that is why many of the churches there are termed Norman.

With the weasel in my arms I walked inside the great stone structure, stopped, took a deep breath, walked from the narthex down the steps into the nave and sat down in one of the wooden chairs. A sudden and simultaneous sense of history, suffering, acceptance and serenity came over me. The walls might have, but did not, whisper. I looked up and saw the spandrels with low-relief sculpture and what I thought of as basket-weave on the walls just before the clerestory—-all of which I loved and all of which remained the same each time I returned, creating a sense of perpetuity. A beam of sunlight, radiating down through one window, bathed Lauren's head, though nothing else, in a flaxen light. I watched minute dust particles dancing around above her head, but oblivious, she slept. Perhaps she felt the sun's warmth.

We left the cathedral and walked to the market where I bought the tiny shrimp called *petite grises*—the kind that you pop off the head, then crunch up the body, legs, shell and all. They were salty and delicious, and I often thought of them in the States, and always made a point of eating them along with the *bulots* and *bigorneaux* the sea snails, that I likewise couldn't find in America. As I snapped off each small head, I threw it down on the pavement for Lauren to snatch up. She was beside herself with gastronomic pleasure. We walked along this way until my entire shrimp bag was empty.

I smiled and nodded to the old ladies in the street. Here, away from Paris, I saw pleasant, happy, little, white-headed ladies, with deep, creviced facial lines—but smile creases, not frown lines. When the squalls blew in I watched them, valiantly pushing along, clinging to the wall, and trying not to blow away with the wind.

From Bayeux we drove to the church of Cerisy-le-Forêt, where Lauren rolled around in the grass outside and then marched right up to the altar inside, and lay down. We visited seventeenth-century Balleroy, designed by Mansart, and then, dusk coming on, set out in search of the little church of Thaon. I never have known its name except to call it that, but I have always loved it. I knew only to look for a dirt road off of the secondary road we were on, the D 170, but then my memory kept playing tricks, and where I thought it should appear it didn't. But we found the dirt road which, different from my remembered version, was no more than a path into the woods, and we parked and began our descent down the trail. Lauren ran up the banks, nose to the ground, sniffing for game. Then around the corner I caught a glimpse of the church. It was as I'd remembered.

I thought about a statue at Dumbarton Oaks in Washington D.C. of a girl and a deer that as children, Amy, Ted, and I had named, why I don't know, the Couplodon. Years later I went back looking for the Couplodon. I walked down to where I knew it would be, but it wasn't. Some things should stay like that. But then later still my mother and I had made another visit. She remembered our fascination with the statue, and walked with me to where it should have been. Still not there. But when we were walking from room to room inside the estate, we stopped, both of us at the same time and said the funny name, aloud. There in the middle of a room sat the Couplodon. There after so many years. Moved inside and domesticated, no longer wild. It was a triumph for my mother and me, but in some ways I wish it had remained a mysterious creation, somewhere between figment and real, tucked away in childhood reverie.

I tugged at Lauren, who was sniffing the ground and didn't care about some old church, and ran the rest of the path. It was nearly dark when we came up beside the church and I knew it'd be locked. I admired its simplicity, its unique belfry and the modillioned cornice running around it. I placed Lauren up on one of the large stone burial vaults to take her picture before the sunlight faded for the day. As I did a Magpie flew by very close to me, and I turned to look for the second one that always followed, but saw nothing. It was all alone. I took Lauren's picture. The flash went off, and for a split second everything nearby burst into light, and then returned to dusk again.

"Come on Lauren, let's go." I wanted to get to our hotel.

Chapter 20

We pulled up to the Hôtel de la Marine beside the Musée du Débarquement in Arromanches. In our room the window looked out onto the beach and the sea and the artificial ports called Mulberries used in the D-day invasion. I was tired and I knew Lauren was too. We had a quick dinner downstairs in the lovely dining room then came back upstairs to sleep, the sound of the surf filling our dreams.

In the morning after *café au lait*, *croissant* and *tartines*, we got in the car and headed west along the coast. First stop, Omaha Beach and the American cemetery. Dogs are strictly forbidden at the cemetery, but there was no way I was not going to take Lauren. For anyone who has not been, the American cemetery is quite simply one of the most heart-rending sights: over nine thousand tiny white Carrara marble crosses, with a few stars-of-David mixed in too, against the greenest grass I have ever seen. I get goose bumps every time I go. We stood at the edge of the grass and paid reverent respect then turned to gaze out to the English Channel far below. I scooped Lauren up in my arms, stepped over the fence and started the lengthy walk down to the shore, Omaha Beach.

LAUREN AND I sit on this enormous expanse of sand alone, save for the seagulls who squawk as they glide by above us. I try to think. June 6, 1944. Now, lovers stroll hand in hand along this gorgeous beach where young men of eighteen stepped off into freezing water then walked into machine-gun fire. Down the road at the Point de Hoc the specially trained Rangers miraculously captured the position by assault. At dawn on the 6th of June, they scaled the high limestone cliffs, heavily defended by the Germans, with ropes and ladders, but not without tremendous losses. Gaping craters testify to the intensity of fighting. St-Laurent-sur-Mer, Colleville-sur-Mer. Now toddlers run along the sand unaware of the footprints of the past. Juno, Gold, Sword—-operational code names until June 1944. Now part of our collective memory. I take off my shoes and socks and walk into the surf. Lauren doesn't want to and she's afraid I'll keep walking and leave her. But I come back, sit down and hold her in my arms for a long time.

Finally I stand, say goodbye to the beach, to all the boys who gave their lives for my own country and for France, and start the hike back up.

WHEN WE REACHED the top again, I realized why we'd been the only ones out on the great stretch of beach. There clearly posted on the correct entry way down to the beach, which was not where we had hopped over, was a sign expressly prohibiting anyone to venture forth because of the *sanglier*. Wild boar. I made Lauren pose in front of the sign for the *sanglier* so Amy would believe me when later I dramatically recounted our adventures.

The D 514 is a wonderfully scenic road that parallels the Normandy coast, popping in and out of hamlets of stone farmhouses. Cows now graze where soldiers once met their deaths. We drove as far as St-Laurent-sur-Mer and sat side by side watching the waves roll in and out.

Back at the Hôtel de la Marine I stood at the window considering the funny Mulberries before getting dressed to go down for dinner. A line of poetry had slipped inside my brain, and now imbedded, it taunted me: "The old lie: *Dulce et decorum est/Pro patria mori*." Different war, but aren't they really all the same?

When I heard the familiar noise, I turned from the window to find Lauren having a seizure, sneezing, licking with her tongue and snapping her jaws without control. I moved to be next to her. She frequently had seizures, most often in the morning, but I rarely worried, for they were small focal seizures. I would pat her and comfort her. I learned if I put pressure on her head, or particularly the insides of her ears, I could get the seizures to stop. But this one seemed different. I put my fingers inside her ears and rubbed. Her compulsive snapping subsided, but when I removed my fingers she started up again. I could do nothing. Fifteen minutes later she was fine again.

The Maître d' led us over to a little table next to the window. I ordered oysters and a bottle of Gros Plant. Lauren sat beside me eating bites of bread. She looked so beautiful that evening. I peered out the window—the tide was far out. When my sole arrived I shared it equally with her.

After dinner I took her out to the beach, black in its darkness, and ran at full speed along the wet sand. She ran too, her dog tracks imprinted on shore. I walked out to the surf, while Lauren hung back, and touched my hands to the cold water. We turned around and, the murky sea behind, the hotel looked inviting with its windows all alit.

Back up in our hotel room, I opened the window so I could hear the surf and smell the salt, then lay back against the headboard with my book. Lauren, pooped, fell immediately asleep at my side. I knew I wouldn't read. I was still thinking of Omaha Beach, still uncomfortable with all those visible ironies.

On our way back to Caen to catch the train, we stopped at the Mémorial de la Paix (Memorial to the Peace), a manipulative, yet excellent museum that traces history from 1918 to the present, with presentations of the Battle of Normandy and the liberation of France from Nazi forces. The D-day invasion is dramatically illustrated by means of simultaneous projection of the Allied and German newsreels onto a giant screen. I watched the young boys slaughtered on the very beach where Lauren and I had sat the day before. Lauren, not allowed in museums, lay quietly, undetected, in her bag by my side. It was just another film to her, but she was beside me.

When the film ended, we headed back to Paris.

Chapter 21

Those were the happy days in Paris, the days filled with beauty and sunshine, contentment and companionship. Mitterand was president and Paris was the undisputed capital of culture.

When winter arrived that year it seemed colder than ever. The skies turned gray, apparently permanently, and I bought Lauren a coat in Louis Vuitton colours. Amy sent her one too, but I called Amy's the Christmas coat and reserved it only for fancy occasions. It was red velvet with green fur trim.

Even though the apartment was cold, I put Lauren in a coat only when we went outside walking, and even then only when bitterly cold. During the day, when I'd work, I'd look over to the sofa and see her curled in a tight ball, her nose tucked up under her tail.

"Lauren, like that little wisp of a tail is really going to do you any good." And I'd laugh at the sight, get up and fix a worn, wool blanket all around her, letting her nose poke out. She'd open her eyes for the briefest of moments in thanks, heave a sigh and return to sleepland.

We walked as much as ever, but I had to make sure to wash Lauren's paws with warm water after each outing, as the salt from the street could burn her pads.

Some evenings were melancholy, yet in a moving way as Paris can be. The air damp and cold, we'd descend underground and get on the métro and feel the stuffy warmth. I loved Paris in the winter, for it was in winter that I first visited the city. When I think of Paris I think of gray skies, cold air and leafless trees. I loved to walk the streets at dusk and watch the lights come on in the apartment buildings. I liked to peer in restaurants and cafés and see the people cozy and content. I would look up to the street lamps and imagine a time before my time when each would have been lit every night by hand.

Chapter 22

One morning we woke as usual. I peered out the window; the city streets looked ashen. Roland was nowhere in sight. Jimmy was standing on the square surveying the preliminary café activity. I took Lauren out and when she caught sight of him she charged forth to the end of her leash to play as usual. He waved his tail when he saw her and I lifted her up over the fence surrounding the fountain, letting her loose to run and chase him. Around and around they went until abruptly Lauren stopped, then started to cough. Looking disappointed Jimmy sniffed her, then leaped out over the railing and trotted away.

"Okay Lauren, let's go," I figured she was just worn out from racing around. I lifted her back over the black railing, put her on the pavement and the coughs subsided. But as we enjoyed our daily activities, a stroll through the Luxembourg, a visit to the *boulangerie*, a trip to the post office, I noticed her intermittently coughing as if she had something stuck in her throat she couldn't rid. When we returned to the apartment, I worked at my desk and Lauren slept on the sofa. *Plus que ça change....*

That evening I had a date with Giles. We'd been seeing each other casually and tonight I'd invited him to a bistro I was reviewing, near the Bon Marché department store.

As we walked in I noticed several tables filled with Japanese tourists and realized I couldn't now claim it as my discovery. We were ushered past the front tables to the area behind, and when we were seated elbow to elbow with the French, I was relieved for I'd made the reservation with my thick American accent. Giles was dressed to the nines as only the French or Italian can, in a dark Dior suit, Stephane Kélian shoes, his slightly longish brown hair falling just across his face. Lauren trailed along after us, thrilled by the smell of food, anticipating what was to come.

Giles ordered a bottle of 1978 Charmes-Chambertin, my favorite year for burgundy.

"Kay," he, too, pronounced it 'Key.' "I ham going to get you quite drunk tonight," he teased. "You need it."

"Is it that obvious?" I smiled at him.

"You never hide en-a-thing, do you? Eet must be ver American. Zuh French air not like zat."

"I know no other way."

"I like eet."

"That's nice."

"I'm still going to get you drunk."

"Ladies do not get drunk."

"Ah-hah! What about zat evening at zhe Cavados bar?"

"That was before I became a lady."

He laughed. And so did I.

"Giles."

"*Oui?*"

"I think I'm already *pompette*."

"*Non, non tu n'es pas pompette*." But he smiled seductively. *Pompette* means tipsy. All the words to describe this altered state induced by alcohol are cute: *pompette*, tipsy, tiddly. The French also have an expression, *entre les deux vins* which means 'between two wines.' The words for the next stage of intoxication are less cute.

"*Mais qu'est-ce que j'ai faim. J'ai vachement faim.*"

When I spoke French I realized the tremendous significance of language, far beyond simply a way to communicate. French was not only different words and pronunciations, but a completely different mentality and way of thinking and being. There is more than an ocean's difference between *la mentalité française* and the American mentality. When I spoke French, my thought process changed. This was one reason I have never been a fan of reading in translation, especially poetry for, as Paul Valery liked to point out, fidelity to meaning alone is a kind of betrayal. But sometimes, if you don't read Russian for instance, there's no alternative.

The woman next to us blew blue-gray smoke out of a Jane Morris mouth that longed for a pomegranate. I hated the French habit of smoking between courses, but when Giles lit up, the smoke looked sexy coming out from between his lips. And when he offered me one, I accepted. Quite suddenly I wanted to go home with him. I had not been with anyone since Jason and my brain, or was it my body, was telling me it was about time lest I turn into an amoeba or some other asexual bit of protoplasm.

"A consummation devoutly to be wished," I said aloud.

"What eeze zat?" he asked innocently.

"It means—" I stopped. As if reading my thoughts he raised his eyes up slowly from his plate, said nothing, and smiled. I smiled back. There are few moments as exhilarating as that one when, seated across from a man at dinner, you realize you're going to be taken to his bed. I wondered how Lauren would feel about this and I looked to her sitting next to me on her own chair. She too was staring in Giles' direction, though it was not to his lips Lauren gazed but to his plate, which still held the last remnants of lamb. When we finished eating, I asked Giles if he wanted a *digestif* and he said no. We couldn't get in a taxi fast enough.

Giles de Gasté lived on the fashionable avenue Foch with neighbors the likes of Caroline Grimaldi. The cut green grass of his apartment building and the trees and gardens surrounding it made me think I was anywhere but in a city. It was posh with a capital P and immediately I thought of Ted.

"Know the derivation of the word posh?" He asked me once.

"No."

"Well, when the English used to go to India, they would always request the port side going over and the starboard on the return, so the sun wouldn't get them. They were the well-to-do ones of course. So Port side Over, Starboard Home, POSH. But today it'd be SOPH so reverent is our worship of the sun." And he started calling things SOPH and no one knew what he was talking about.

But Giles' building was nothing special; his neighbors had golf courses on top of them. It was stupefying the money some people had, when over in the eighteenth *arrondissement*, on the rue de la Goutte d'Or, poverty beckoned to the North Africans in the same way it had to Gervais Lantier a century ago.

I wanted, and yet I didn't want, to delay what we were about to do for as long as I could. There is a stage at which, wouldn't it be nice if you could always keep it....

Chapter 23

In the morning I lay beside Giles with Lauren tucked into my back on the other side. She had paid our exertions no attention and quickly dropped off to sleep, content to be by my side. Unlike some dogs who are wary of strangers, Lauren seemed to like all dogs and most people.

I looked to the curled brown leaves on the big oak tree out Giles' bedroom window, and realized that long after his handsome face had turned old and wrinkled, long after he and I had ceased, the oak would stand budding each spring and shedding its leaves in the fall.

I'd been awake thinking for a while when he languidly turned over and smiled at me. I would have liked to have passed a leisurely morning, but I was becoming increasingly concerned, for Lauren had not taken and needed her pills. I explained this to Giles, declining even his offer of coffee, and with a grace I was unaccustomed to finding in all previous men, he told me he understood. Lauren and I walked out the fluid Art Nouveau front door, greeted by the morning sun.

Once outdoors on the spongy grass Lauren raced to the end of her leash and started investigating the ground and trees. I inhaled the air deeply, suddenly glad to be outside. The sky was a soft morning blue and the sun shown down.

"Come on Lauren, let's run!" We raced toward the Arc de Triomph along the grass, me admiring the apartment buildings, Lauren jerking abruptly to a stop if she thought she saw food. When we got to the great arch we walked around and descended the stairs to the métro. I lifted Lauren into the train and held her in my arms. And again I noticed her coughing.

Then I noticed her breathing was faster than usual.

The métro ride from Charles-de-Gaulle-Etoile to Place Monge, with a change at Palais Royal, takes about twenty-five minutes. I would have sworn I was trapped on that train, Lauren in my arms, for over an hour. By the time we were half way home, Lauren was having a hard time breathing at all. Her nostrils flared out and her sides heaved in and out rapidly. She cough, cough, coughed, then gagged. All that I had heretofore felt then labeled as "fear" in my short life on earth would have to be redefined. People stared at my dog, then glanced at me, but said nothing.

Palais Royal, Pont Neuf. I knew them by heart. Why was this train taking so long? Pont Mairie. Get *in* people. Close doors. Sully Morland. Stop. Out, people out. Shut doors. *Move* train. Jussieu.

Place Monge. Doors please open.

With Lauren tight in my arms, I pushed past the deluge, ran two steps at a time up the escalator that Lauren so valiantly always walked up, brushed by ladies pulling shopping bags with wheels, and into the apartment.

Hurriedly I gave Lauren all her medication. Yet I was certain it was not from lack of medicine that she was reacting the way she was; these pills treated her seizures. This was something else. I phoned Dr. Cauzinelle, while Lauren sat straining to breath and wheezing on the sofa. I comforted her as best I could, but she couldn't lie down. She couldn't put her head down without hindering her breathing.

Dr. Cauzinelle is not in today, the voice said. Would I like to make an appointment? No, this is an emergency. What do I do? Calmly and *slowly* she gave me the name of a veterinary hospital. I scribbled down the address then telephoned for a taxi. Oh please, have one ready right now. I was put on hold and that inane recording runs through my head still, "*Alpha Taxi, Bonjour. Veuillez patientez, s'il vous plaît. Notre service...*" Then, a voice. Taxi in "*cinq minutes.*" Oh Lauren, oh Lauren, oh Lauren. I held her on the couch.

When the taxi pulled up I told the jovial driver to drive as fast as he knew how and I would pay him well. I did not want to make conversation. He did as bidden. I didn't watch where we were going. Once there, I carried Lauren in and had to fill out forms and again wait. Then a young man told me to follow him into an examining room and I explained to him what had happened. Lauren was shivering and breathing hard. He took her temperature, 105.

"*Oui, c'est vrai, elle est malade.*" He took her from me and said to come back tomorrow morning. Come back tomorrow morning? Let's try again. I said I wanted to know what was going on and that I'd stay right here, thank you. Okay, okay, half condescending, half indulgent, smile. I sat. I thumbed through *Le Nouvel Observateur*, but I couldn't read. I looked at the pictures in *Paris Match*. I just wanted to see her. Why did hospitals never let you see your loved ones? What if they died on the operating table? Wouldn't it be better for both you and them if you'd been there? I would behave myself. I wasn't the hysterical type. I'd experienced too much in life to get dramatic about its vicissitudes.

The advertisement for dog bones that clean the teeth is engraved in my brain. I watched the citizens of Paris walk in and out with cats and dogs, sometimes a bird. And then the woman with the tiny monkey who kept saying, "He dies little," meaning he never grows any bigger. Parisians walked in, sometimes in agitated states, yelling in accusation, often in fashionable clothes with great self-assurance. But I could concentrate on nothing save what might be happening to Lauren behind those shut doors.

When a Chihuahua tiptoed in on a leash, I could hear Ted, "Rodent on a string."

Time passed. Another doctor came out to the waiting room.

"*Madamoiselle Pfaltz?*"

"*Oui, c'est moi.*"

He told me Lauren was recovering, but was still very sick. It was hard trying to understand the medical terms he used, not to mention the fact that they were in French. I kept asking him to repeat himself and he did so patiently, explaining to me that Lauren had aspirated pneumonia. She was now hooked up to IVs for fluid and liquid antibiotics. She still had a high temperature and was weak, but by evening she might be okay to go home.

"But why?" I asked.

"We don't know yet. She is old, yes?"

I told him I didn't really know, that I had found her. "Could I see her?" No, he said, that might upset her and she needed to remain calm. But she'll be okay? Yes, he reassured me.

Relief.

Was relief the same as happiness? I was *happy*. There is a kind of paramount happiness that can only be felt or occur after anguish. The reverse of suffering. I understood this in the way I understood death's opposition but requisition to life.

Hours later, the same vet came out and beckoned me to the examining room. He held up three containers of pills and told me what they each were and how to administer them. Then a woman walked in with Lauren in her arms. Lauren looked bleary, like she'd had a hard night out, but she flapped her tail when she saw me. I took her in my arms and she started to cough uncontrollably. She was excited to see me, they explained.

I thanked them and left and as I did the doctor said, *"Bon courage. Elle était une très bonne cliente."*

In the back of the taxi I held Lauren in my arms and stroked her head. She was here, and I felt I could never get enough of her. Her breathing was strained, but she slept in my arms, exhausted, the little blue bandage on her leg where the IV had been making her look all the more vulnerable.

I kept her on antibiotics for two weeks and never left her side. I saw no movies, cooked in, and read many books with the weasel curled up beside me. After the first couple days on the medication she looked and acted just like before, except she had a slight continual cough.

I thought all was well. But when three weeks and two days to date from her first pneumonia attack she contracted another, I knew something was wrong.

The fear was the same, but so was the procedure and the hospital, so at least I knew what I was doing. When Lauren came home from the veterinary hospital this time, I knew I would leave Paris. I wanted the reassurance of my own language and my own country. I wanted the vets who had nursed her away from death and starvation. I called the countess and I called Giles. I called Amy and explained my decision to her. Then I called my editor and boss stating that I hoped it would be a temporary leave.

In the evening we went out for one last meal in Paris.

Chez Pento was a little restaurant very close to me, but not so close that it got caught up in the mediocre food syndrome that my neighborhood's tourist draw fostered. I fell in love with it for the *foie gras* and *confit de canard*, and also because it was cheap. The staff all fell in love with Lauren. We became known at many restaurants, but, if I were to loose my memory, Chez Pento would stay etched in my mind somehow when the others slipped out.

This evening we walked in to Chez Pento and kissed cheek to cheek. One of the waiters grabbed Lauren and, holding her high in the air slowly brought her down clasping her to his chest chanting, "*Ah, je suis content. Maintenant, je suis content. Qu'est-ce que tu veux manger ce soir, ma petite, eh? Tout? Tu veux tout? Ah oui, je sais. Comme toujours. Mais, bien sûr, ma cherie. Bien sûr.*" He talked directly to her.

We dined together side by side, like an old couple so familiar and at peace with one another as to be content in comfortable silence. Her devotion never wavered and by now I was accustomed to it. But strangers were not. She would raise her head, tilting it slightly and simply gaze at me.

Chez Pento filled with smoke as more and more diners arrived. I noticed the heavy gold jewelry and tanned hands of women attired in Thierry Mugler and agnès b. An American couple walked in and I picked them for such right away. Later in the evening I could hear the woman say, trying to be quiet, but not succeeding—it's the tone:

"Harold, look there's a dog over there. That's dirty. Harold, let's go. The French are strange." Harold only grunted in response.

I think Harold's wife was probably dirtier than Lauren ever could be, and certainly less polite. Lauren had impeccable manners. This woman did not. Compassion, tolerance and respect towards others, even canine others, count for something.

The hum of voices, the clatter of plates, the hustle and bustle of the bistro, with its tarnished mirrors and Toulouse-Lautrec prints hanging above, all welded together to both warm and thrill me.

We were again happy and we stayed for hours.

Chapter 24

I loved Paris, but was happy to be leaving for a while. I needed the country. I missed the silence. I missed the gentle mountains, the stars and the moon, that I saw so seldom in the city. I missed the seasons of Virginia: the cool, crisp air of October; the breathtaking colors of red and gold; the brisk and bracing cold of December; the winter sunsets and bare, skeletal trees; then those first tentative days of spring so filled with promise, the promise of the redbud and the apple trees; and the soft, decadent warmth of summer evenings. I missed the sounds and smells of the country: the peepers at dusk, the rustle of the wind in the leaves, the dawn chorus as I awoke to each new day, and the late-afternoon air perfumed with honeysuckle, my earliest remembered smell.

It's odd, but it was the city that taught me to fully appreciate the country. Now, when I'm in Paris, a tree decked in full foliage or the notes of a city bird can bring me the sensation of standing in the silence of the countryside. I no longer think of the Parisian parks and gardens as sculpted bits of manmade symmetry, but accept them for the natural panoply they try to assert despite man's intervention.

I rented a small white farmhouse in Nelson County, one of Virginia's poorest counties, but in my mind also one of Virginia's most beautiful. The area was magical—it had something beyond beauty. It neighbored Albemarle County where the rest of my family lived.

I sublet my apartment in Paris, but the money only paid to keep it. It didn't provide me with income.

The drive to the vets in Earlysville from my new place took me nearly an hour. The technicians took X-rays to see what was going on in those lungs of Lauren's. They weren't a fluidy mess the way they had been when she was in the middle of pneumonia, but then she was still on the antibiotics. As Dr. John held up the radiographs, he pointed to the left, lower lobe and said it was scared and would probably never operate in its full capacity again. But it was what he said next that sent a chill through my body.

"Now I think there's really no reason for alarm," he said, "but it seems here her heart is enlarged more than it should be. I think it wouldn't hurt to see a specialist."

"What does that mean?" A thousand questions raced in my mind. They didn't know just now why it should be enlarged or what it meant. We'd probably need to see a specialist.

When we got home, I called Amy. As always she could read the panic level in my voice.

"But she's always had a big heart, Kay."

"I know."

"Come on," she coaxed. "She'll be okay... Try not to get constipated over it."

"I think it's consternated."

"Don't be semantic."

"Pedantic."

"Kay!"

"Bye sis."

I was smiling when I hung up the phone. I looked at Lauren. While Amy had only been trying to console me, I knew what she said was true. Lauren had the biggest heart of any dog I'd ever known.

That night before I went to sleep, I walked outside and stood beneath the stars. I always wished on the stars. I looked up, made the same wish I always did, then added a special wish. Then I started to laugh, remembering one time with Amy as children.

"Kay, it's cloudy tonight, you can't wish on the stars."

"But there's one. Look. It's peeking out of the clouds just for me. That means my wish is sure to come true."

"Kay." Her voice was patient.

"What?"

"That's an airplane."

I looked back up into the sky.

"Well go ahead, then. You never know, maybe it works with airplanes too."

But my wish hadn't come true, so from that day forward, I always made sure that the stars I wished on were stationary, unless of course they were falling stars. But that's a different story.

Chapter 25

Virginia was lazily drifting into summer and when one evening I first heard the cicadas begin their funny song, it was music to my city-starved ears. If winter brought cold weather tempting Lauren's pneumonia, summer brought hazards such as snakes and bees. Copperheads abounded. I once found one residing in my bathroom. Lauren was bitten by a snake, but I think the snake that bit her was less venomous. Her nose swelled up like a beach ball and I rushed her to the emergency vets. She was in pain, but she never once cried. Amy said of course she did it to get sympathy food.

It was on one summer day, after a trip to the vet that I decided to have Lauren's portrait painted. At the time I didn't realize, in commissioning the painting, that I was trying to hold on to her forever. I just knew that the urge to have a great, big beautiful oil that I would hang in a gilt frame ("the gaudier, the better," said Amy) above the fireplace was tremendous. Because Amy knew all the horse and dog people who'd had their own pets painted, I had her research it, and she found me a painter for a good price. The price I paid Amy, however, was steeper. I had to endure her frequent enquiries, disguised ostensibly as interest, but always followed by squeals of laughter, concerning *The Portrait of the Weasel*.

Chapter 26

"Hey kid, don't worry about it. Stay as long as you need. You've done a good job, I'm not going to hire anyone else." Bobby Beckford was a true Virginia gentleman. I thanked him. If he didn't understand about Lauren, I knew Felicia did. I was about to hang up when he said, "Hey kid, how many movies you see, you haven't yet reviewed?"

"Quite a few, sir."

"Write them up. You don't have a pea brain. You can remember. Don't have to be on French soil to write them up."

I was speechless. It would mean a trickle of income when I had none, facing mounting vet bills.

"Restaurants too, if you think you can. That's a bit more dicey. Up to you."

"Yes sir."

"Right then." He hung up.

I was in no hurry to return to Paris, for I wanted to understand what was going on with Lauren and why. While I knew Lauren loved Paris, walking the streets, smelling the smells, and going out to eat, I also saw how much she must have missed her native Virginian countryside, just like me, for she would race around on her own, doing "the whirlies," then twist upside down in the grass with, I swear, what looked like a smile on her face. Some days she'd come inside and greet me with not only brown feet where white used to be, but also a brown nose in place of her normal black. She looked so pleased with herself, and I'd go out in the yard and find a giant hole in my nice grass. I knew the unpolluted air was good for us both. Lauren loved both Paris and Virginia, but most of all she loved any place I was.

Just as in Paris, we did everything together. I couldn't take her in restaurants. I tried; I argued with waiters, with managers, with owners, but rules were rules. Sometimes we could sit outside, but it wasn't the same as in Paris. Some shops allowed her. Most did not. She did go through the carwash with me, scared at first until I explained everything that was going on, and then she quieted down and watched out the splattered windows in earnest.

Often I went riding with Amy and Lauren kept up with the horses. It was great exercise. On this morning I rode beside Amy on one of her several thoroughbreds in the early light. Delicate, cottony clouds, the first of the day, drifted indifferently above.

"She loves you Kay." Amy said watching Lauren. "Look at her down there, looking up at you."

"Yeah. And you know, I've never loved anything the way I love her, and the thing is, I know I never will again."

"Kay, please. It's too early."

"No, I mean it," I said this seriously and Amy, hearing my tone, responded with a sigh.

"I hope you will."

"Amy, but the thing is I don't want to wake up one day and not be able to remember her. Not remember how it was. That would be the worst thing."

"You won't. That won't ever happen."

"But time has such power."

"It has the power to heal. What will happen is this. When she dies you'll feel horrible pain." Amy spoke from much experience. "But one day you'll wake and instead of feeling the horrible pain you're so accustomed to feeling when you think about her, instead you'll feel joy. You'll smile to yourself and say her name out loud. Her memory will bring you great happiness. And you'll feel rich and full inside because you'll know you loved something the very best you could."

I was amazed. She didn't lecture me on the futility or, more accurately, the harmfulness of worrying about things that hadn't yet happened. She didn't start in on the starving Ethiopians.

"Amy, I thought you didn't believe in all that stuff. I thought that was my line."

"I just don't talk about it. But I'll tell you what I believe in. I believe in love that transcends the ordinary day to day. Love that transcends life. Love that transcends suffering. I've observed you and I see you've found this kind of love with the form there." She nodded to Lauren.

"She's my life."

"I'd forgotten you were a drama major in school."

"Funny."

"I hope you don't go around talking to other people about her the way you do with me, because…"

"I don't. I save it all for you."

"Thanks."

"You know the Arabs have a word for it."

"A word for what?"

"*Hiaty*. It means my life." But before Amy could voice her disgust, I said quickly, "Sis… when she goes, I'll have her cremated. Then when I go, I want to be cremated and mixed with her and scattered in the Luxembourg gardens. Will you do that for me?"

"Kay. I'm two years older than you. I expect I'll already be dead." Amy was very logical. "Hey how's *The Portrait of the Weasel* coming?"

"Almost done," I said quickly, trying not to encourage her.

Without warning, Amy broke into a canter and was soon gliding over a brush jump. I was about to follow when I saw there was no way over or around for Lauren. I stopped, dismounted, picked Lauren up, leaped back on and cantered forward.

"One, two, three, unto the breach!" Together, Lauren and I sailed over the jump. I didn't think. I just did it, like I had to. And I knew from that moment forward that that's how I'd react in any situation, grave or comical, concerning my dog. I still have the scar on my elbow where, instead of tripping and falling on Lauren, I once opted to fall against the window, crashing into it and shattering the glass. Amy's typical remark, "Careful Kay, there's a fine line between bravery and stupidity."

Then the time in a London tube station, when a Yorkshire terrier was knocked onto the track before the approaching train. I jumped down reacting, not thinking. I handed the frightened Yorkie back to an overwhelmed older lady who, it turned out, could never have leapt down to the track, even if she'd had the nerve to do so. I didn't take the money she kept thrusting towards me, thinking only somehow that I'd saved Lauren.

Amy loved my feat over the jump. Perplexed, for she'd momentarily forgotten about Lauren—-the dogs she had out were all big enough to jump over—Amy hollered out, "You looked good. Both of you."

She called her dogs and ordered them to walk close to her, for there was a deer carcass ahead.

"You know, they're now saying that certain meats cause cancer. I *ask* you."

"Well, Lauren never met a food she couldn't eat," I boasted.

"Yeah, I know, the catfish of the dog world. Still watch out, that'd be all you need." She started to smile at me, but suddenly her face altered and she visibly shook. "God. The weirdest chill just ran down my spine and all over me. Did you feel anything?"

"Nope."

"It's gone now. Strange."

The sun was slipping behind the mountain range when we turned around to walk back the long way. Lauren was on my lap. It was time to go home and eat.

Chapter 27

Lauren rarely barked, except when she picked up the scent of rabbits or deer. Ninety percent of Lauren was nose. Ten percent was sight. I learned a lot about hunting by observing her. And I came to love that sound she made more than any other. "Rwoaf, rwoaf, rwoaf." It was husky like she had been hard at the cigarettes. Only later did I discover why.

She didn't bark, but boy, did she let me know when she wanted food, which was most of the time. Usually these antics started well before the hour of the Feeding Frenzy, which was supposed to be around six o'clock. She'd start pestering me two, sometimes three hours before it was time. If I was sitting at my desk working she would come right up next to the chair and hook her little white feet over the arm rail. She'd stare up excitedly, trembling, while squeezing the muscles in her head. The first time I told Amy about how the muscles in her head contracted when she became unduly excited, my sister laughed me out of the room. Not until one of the vets told Amy about her own dog who did the same thing, did Amy accept it as fact. But it didn't stop her from laughing at me.

When Lauren really felt she deserved a meal, she'd sit right beside me wherever I was and cock her head back over her shoulder, role her big brown eyes, and simply gaze at me. I found this display of hers quite cute, and she knew it. If I had fed her an early dinner for some reason, she tried to coax me into a second one. If her persistent gazing didn't do the trick, she ingratiated herself with me by walking around on my lap, or my stomach if I was reading reclining, then she would stand on top of me, and the same thing: throw her head back dramatically, role her eyes and direct her gaze at me.

"Lauren, don't pull that Bosnia-dog look on me."

If her tactics failed—and mind you she'd persevere for a long time—she'd do the one thing that got me every time. She would start by waving one white leg in the air, then two white legs, then she would rear back on her hind legs and continue waving the front ones around. Then (intentionally or unintentionally I don't know) she'd begin to fall backward, for she was never well-balanced. And that did it, I'd give her a biscuit.

Life-form or not, she was smart about getting what she wanted. I'd walk into the kitchen, where I might have left a tiny scrap of bread lying on the counter, and there would be Lauren, up on a chair or whatever she could find. There she'd be about to launch her body across the room to the unsuspecting bread. Once I'd left a large bowl of spaghetti sitting out on the counter far above her reach. That didn't stop her. Somehow she managed to slide one of the kitchen chairs all the way across the room till it was directly under the counter where the pasta sat. She then hoped up, and up again onto the counter. What she didn't do was push the chair back into place around the table. Probably too stuffed on noodles to expend herself. So when I returned I didn't have to be Sherlock Holmes to figure it out, it was all right there: empty spaghetti bowl, chair next to the counter, blimp masquerading as dog.

At night we slept side by side. I frequently had to vie for space in the bed because Lauren stretched her little body out and took up all the room. During dreams, she'd kick me with her little feet that smelled sweet from sleep. And by the morning I'd be lying on a tiny strip of mattress, eight inches across, and Lauren would have two thirds of the bed. As the years passed, she snored more and more, louder than the fattest man could have possibly. Amy was convinced this was why I remained single. One night exasperated, I pushed her muzzle shut and said, "Lauren, I don't want to hear you snore anymore." Then I paused, thought briefly about my words, and silently prayed for that special music in my ear to go on for a very long time. I leaned over and whispered to her, "You go right ahead and snore for as long as you possibly can." And she did too. Her snoring never bothered me again.

I always took Lauren's collar off at night for her to sleep unencumbered. Then I'd slip my watch off and place it inside her collar. It was a ritual, like brushing one's teeth, and every morning I'd wake to find them both there resting together.

She'd curl up and fit snugly in the crook of my arm. I'd hold her this way and feel I was protecting her and would never let anything happen to her. And thinking of Scarlett O'Hara, I'd tell her, "Lauren, you'll never be starving again." Sometimes when I held her tight at night I'd think of all the other dogs who'd never known the comfort of love. I'd think of strays who were euthanized, the dogs and cats who were unloved, abused...the chickens and turkeys, cows and pigs, goats, sheep, lambs, lobsters, crabs butchered, often cruelly, merely for our consumption; the rabbits tested upon, like the beagles, for our use of drugs. Then from domestic thoughts, I moved on to empathize with all the abused donkeys in Asia. A streak of guilt would flash through me for not only eating, but deliriously reveling in *foie gras*. Each time, I would vow to change, and I'd hold Lauren closer trying to comfort all the animals with my love for one.

Chapter 28

One morning I discovered a spider had spun her web and sat large, right in its center. As the web was next to the cupboard door, it interfered with the door's opening. I knew I would have to destroy this delicate filigree, but couldn't bring myself to do it. It was drizzling outside, I rationalized. I'll do it tomorrow—I couldn't throw the spider out in the rain. The next day by accident I damaged the web when going into the cupboard. I felt bad. But it was done.

That same morning I fed Lauren and walked outside with her. It was still lightly raining, and I tilted my head back and let the drops hit my face. When I looked down at Lauren she was stumbling like she was drunk. I took several quick steps back from her, then called.

"Lauren, come here." She came towards me then veered off to the left.

"Lauren, come!" She straightened her course, but veered off again. Then she gave up and headed, crookedly for the door. She shook the rain off her coat, and as she did, she fell over on her side.

"Lauren!"

I was at her side; she staggered up.

"Lauren, what is it?" *Why* can't they talk to us? But they do. I looked into her deep, brown eyes and saw immediately what I hadn't seen before. One eye looked a little swollen and had none of the sparkle the other one had.

I picked her up, and dialed the vets.

Once I'd arrived, I found the vets were stumped. They watched her trying to walk around. They watched her fall if she cut a corner too sharply. They ran tests and found nothing. I could only hear bits and pieces as they consulted amongst themselves.

"...forcing the equilibrium to be off, but what—"

"Inner ear disease will often—"

"Tumor...."

"—of the brain."

"—only thing that would cause...."

"We'd better move quickly."

They phoned Virginia Tech, a veterinary school, and made an appointment for Lauren to have a CT scan that afternoon.

Virginia Tech was three hours away in Blacksburg. When I arrived I had to explain first to the vet-school student and again to the doctor all of Lauren's problems, from the seizures to the pneumonia attacks for which she was still on Baytril, to possible G.I. disease and now this, whatever it was. I was impatient and disliked explaining her case, or cases, to the students, but I should have been grateful, for it helped keep the cost down. When Dr. Dyer, the head neurologist, finally breezed in fresh as a daffodil from the field, I was relieved for she was the best there was and I knew too she'd treated many of Amy's dogs.

I knew the drill all too well: "Come back in the afternoon." Afternoon meant around five or six o'clock, not two or three. Yet I always returned at two or three, taking some comfort in being near my dog even if I couldn't see her. I could never eat or read much anyway. I tried, but my thoughts riveted toward one small, tri-color dog under anesthesia. Lately she'd been put under so many times. It was hard on a body. Would she make it through this time?

A woman walked in with a vizsla, graceful and sleek. "Come on Sheba." They sat down next to me.

"Hello, you're beautiful," I said to the vizsla.

"She's here for hip surgery," the woman explained to me, telling me all about her many medical problems. I wanted to tell her about Lauren, but the words didn't come. Then seeking comfort I reached to stroke Sheba. But the head was the wrong size.

Sometime just before six pm, Karen Dyer came out, sat down beside me and started to talk. I could see why my sister liked her so much. She seemed to genuinely care for each dog, and I trusted Lauren in her competent hands.

"Lauren will be out soon. She's still recovering."

I let out held breath.

"We have good news," she continued. "At least I think you'll consider it good." She laughed a little, for nothing was ever easy concerning Lauren.

"First of all, there's no tumor."

My face muscles must have relaxed, for she smiled.

"We took an EEG. Her brain waves aren't normal, but there's no reason for alarm."

"What does it mean?"

"Well, it probably has something to do with the seizures. She probably developed all this when she was starving, when she was young. Very likely she had distemper. The thing is, we don't *know* what happened to her."

"I know. We never will." I paused. "Is she in pain?"

"No, not at all. She probably feels a little bit foggy. Just a little bit out of it." I definitely would not repeat this part to Amy. "She may be confused," she continued. "Especially when she's seizing, but she doesn't suffer."

"That being my greatest concern."

"I know."

"But what happened this morning? Why could she barely walk?"

"I'm coming to that. We took blood and we found her thyroid was off. We did a couple other tests to verify. She has a thyroid imbalance. We gave her medication. You should see immediate results. It's quite controllable. Give her one of these every morning." She handed me a container filled with pink pills.

"Soloxine," I read. "Will it interfere with her other drugs."

"No."

Then I remembered something I'd heard. "Distemper? It's untreatable isn't it?"

"Yes. It's probably what caused her to have the seizures. But it doesn't seem to be affecting her now."

"So when she was young, her brain got fried from the virus?"

"Well... yes."

"What does it do if it gets worse?"

"It would attack her brain."

Just then a vet tech walked up with a dog in her arms and placed it on my lap. I forgot my worries as I experienced that moment, the moment when I first see her after the long anxious hours, and she sees me, and I hold her in my arms again. I was to experience that moment again and again.

"Lauren," I said as she looked up at me. Her head and neck were shaved and she was still groggy. She looked awful. Dog-lovers are divided between those who believe dogs do have self-awareness, and those who believe they have little or none. At first with Lauren, I believed the latter. With time, however, I came to see the former was true.

I knew Dr. Dyer had many more dogs to attend and couldn't spend all her time reassuring dog owners that nothing bad would ever happen to their dogs, when she didn't always believe so herself. I thanked her for her help and she bid us both goodbye. I thanked the powers above for the immediate good news and tried not to think about the future just yet.

When we returned late in the evening, I was tired. I fed Lauren first. She had developed the habit of sitting in front of the Feeding Frenzy cabinet (a beat-up, gray, construction in which I kept her food, drugs, rawhides, biscuits and bowl) and staring at it, sometimes for hours at a time like a kid with TV.

"Lauren, think if you stare hard enough, the door will open?"

I went next to the cupboard to feed myself. I reached for the door, then stopped. There before me was the spider web, a brand new one, in the same place. It looked as if nothing had ever happened. I had no idea they could spin them so quickly. I looked at it in awe. It deserved to remain there; I would be careful opening the cupboard door.

I heard the slurping noises at my feet. She was gulping down her food as if nothing had ever happened.

Chapter 29

The Portrait of the Weasel arrived on a rainy day. A maroon minivan came crunching up my driveway, and two men got out. My family, including Lauren, was all assembled as the men carried the oil painting inside wrapped in blankets. The unveiling took place in the dining room. I was nervous, but when the last blanket was removed, everyone gasped. It was her. The painter had gotten it right. The portrait turned out to be not only beautiful, but more important, an almost exact likeness of Lauren. It captured her expression. It captured her soul. I was glad, for I knew I couldn't have hung it had it not been her.[1]

We toasted the painting and Lauren's health, then everyone left. Amy was going out that night with Linda and a bunch of friends. She invited me, but I declined. Sometimes among a group of people I felt the outsider. It was a feeling I'd carried with me all my life, and one that was now compounded the more I did, with the feeling that no one could relate to such experiences. I looked at Lauren. She knew the places I loved, and somehow this knowledge comforted me.

I put the champagne glasses in the sink and took Lauren in my arms and held her up to see her portrait. She gave a puffy little cough, and gazed back at me over her shoulder. I think she sighed and shook her head. I put her down beside me.

[1] Later when this portrait was damaged in a move, my mother painted another, even more beautiful, portrait, which hangs in my house today.

Chapter 30

Lauren always had to be up on something, chair, bed, sofa. She rarely lay on the floor unless she got very hot. On this particular day, I was sitting on the outside step, beside the big cement flower urn. Lauren decided to hop up into the flower pot on its pedestal and lie there, crushing all my pansies, in the sun beside me. I guess she liked the vantage point. Often, from that day on, and especially as she aged, I'd find her up there sleeping in the flower urn. I'd continue to plant various assortments of flowers and she'd continue to squash them all as she slept on them, and I hoped there'd never come a time when my pansies would stand uncrushed, vibrant and healthy.

She also loved to get up on one particular wing chair in the house. It was a hideous green affair I'd picked up in a second-hand shop for twenty-five dollars in attempt to fill the empty house. I needed to buy fabric and have it covered, but I wasn't very good at that sort of thing. Lauren loved that chair. I realized she didn't care that it was ugly. Animals don't. She loved it for what it was—soft and welcoming and comfortable.

There were so many moments in time when I'd stop and look at her and be transfixed to another place—somewhere I was certain I'd never been before, but somewhere reassuringly familiar. Then it would happen more and more frequently, just a fleeting vision and a feeling—that place I see and know we'll go to together, a quiet taste of eternity…

I realized that Lauren's perilous health helped me value life all the more. And I wondered if we can only fully appreciate life when we understand and accept its impermanence.

To say Lauren was "so good," as I'd hear time and again would be to understate. At the vet she'd let her teeth be cleaned, conscious without anesthesia, and she'd lie perfectly still for the ultrasound.

No, Lauren was more than merely "good." Lauren was accepting, patient and trusting; she had good days and bad days, but on the bad days she never complained. She lived each day as it came, in the present, not thinking about the past or worrying about the future. And when I did things to her she didn't like, she chose forgiveness over revenge. The more I observed her, the more I was humbled. I believe she taught me more than a shelf full of self-help books ever could.

There were moments with her when, as on an airplane once, forced into an emergency landing complete with flames, I understood what mothers must feel of their children, what was important to me: her life and little else. The material possessions, we once thought meaningful, cease to hold value.

When she got older she would lie on her side in her chair, but sometimes not fall completely asleep. She'd gaze at me, her eyes never leaving my face, as if to say, "Stay by me. Don't ever go away from me." And I'd say aloud,

"I won't ever leave you Lauren, you know that." Then she'd close her eyes and sleep.

On hot, humid days Lauren would vacate her chair and opt instead to lie on the cold floor tiles. I sat down next to her putting ice cubes all over her head and body for we lived with no air conditioning. Then I'd hold out the cube and let her lick and chew on it. No, it wasn't a cookie, but she felt like she was at least getting to eat something.

Then on poor days—not poor, dreary or poor not feeling well, but poor as in we had no money—to ward off the encroaching pity party, I'd say, "Lauren, I wouldn't give you away for all the money in the world, and there's a lot of money in the world. But there's only one weasel!" And we'd dance around the house singing and boosting each other up.

I never once hit Lauren, yet I frequently had to scold her. She'd grovel real low to the ground like a reptile. I sometimes had a temper, yet it never reared itself around Lauren, even when she deserved it or when she caused me great trouble. I attributed this to unconditional love. I just could never get angry at her, I loved her too much.

How to explain to someone who didn't know, how I felt when I would walk into the room and suddenly see her, sometimes after only minutes? How to explain how I felt when I'd come home at night, having been away all day, and I'd first catch sight of her lying on the back of the sofa watching for me out the window? And there she'd be scraping at the door to get out to see me, jumping up to greet me, then tearing around the yard doing whirlies in pure joy. How to explain how I felt when, sitting at my desk upstairs, I'd hear her step, slower as she aged, and the jingle of her tags as she walked up the stairs to be near me.

Lauren and I were inseparable. She waited for me in the mornings to go downstairs. She watched me work during the day. She came into the room where I was reading. She slept by my side at night.

She had become so much a part of me, I could not imagine life without her.

On the longest day of the year, Lauren and I sat under the big willow tree, waiting till the sun slipped behind the mountains, illuminating cotton candy clouds like someone was shining a big red flashlight from behind. Lauren was singularly round that day, little head, bulging body, having stolen and eaten half a cream-cheese pound cake.

"This is it, Lauren. This is our life." I looked over my shoulder in through the window and saw the ceiling fan spinning lazily in the kitchen. When I looked back the light had already changed. The peepers peeped. Lauren stretched her plump body then rolled in the cut grass. The sun set, the fire flies came out like magic, and I felt like a child again. For that moment I longed to step back into my childhood, but knew the door was forever barred. Everything was still, but I sensed time passing.

Chapter 31

Time stops for no one. Lauren's beautiful brown head and muzzle turned gray with the passing of the years, until one day it seemed I woke and her whole face was white and I couldn't remember her otherwise. Her back which used to be so sleek and black was now streaked with gray. Her sides were mottled-looking, with white more predominant than brown. Sometimes Amy would shriek, "She's so white!" And once I was shocked when, looking through old photographs of her in one of my many albums, I saw her young, all brown and black with the only white her legs and stomach. How ironic that our one constant should be the passage of time.

She no longer bounded upstairs, but walked up carefully one step at a time. She developed an unsightly lump on her eyelid, spots in her eyes, and a wart under her chin, but it didn't matter to me. She could have been hairless and covered in warts—to me she was the most beautiful thing in the world.

Do we automatically find the beloved beautiful? Like a partner we are initially drawn to by physical comeliness, I fell in love with Lauren's picture because I found her so cute. But as in true and lasting love, as opposed to fancy or mere attraction, she remained beautiful even in sickness and old age, in fact, becoming more so. I suppose true beauty is born of love.

On Thanksgiving at my mother's house, Lauren sat up at the table with us, and I thought back to the time when she'd stolen the Beckford's pheasant. Times had changed. We'd all changed. My mother and father looked older, and moved more slowly. Only the mutual respect and admiration we all carried for one another hadn't changed.

Thanksgiving turned into the hustle and bustle and commercialism of Christmas. I ignored the commercialism and focused instead on the nearly six inches of snow that covered most parts of Virginia. Everything shimmered. It was invigorating.

Chapter 32

About a week before Christmas, Amy came over to my house bringing only Bogie. Lauren was overjoyed to see him, and the two old buddies raced around, oblivious to the fact that they were no longer young and spry. We left them to play in the snow and went to the living room. Amy had a new boyfriend, and she was in one of her rare confiding moods. This sounded serious.

The fire blazed and I made two mugs of steaming hot chocolate, the old-fashioned way with real cocoa, not from a packet. Then as Amy described her new love and love affair, I settled myself comfortably back against the sofa, rested my elbow on a plump cushion and listened. And as I listened to my sister talk, observing her face and watching the snowflakes swirl upwards behind her at the window, I realized I didn't miss Paris at all.

"D'you love him?" I asked hopeful.

"I hardly know him. Can you love something unknown?"

"Well, do you love what you know?"

"Yes."

"Well then."

"This may sound odd, but I think he has too much money."

I laughed. You didn't hear that particular statement coming from a woman much these days, or in any day, for that matter. But I understood, for I understood Amy and her tremendous need for independence. And I knew this guy was not just a millionaire, but some multi-gadzillionaire who'd made his money, of all things, from car washes.

"He says he's rich because he "mises" his money."

"Verb."

"Yeah. He says, with a few notable exceptions, the rich mise, while the rest of us economize. That's how they keep their money."

"I mise, you mise, he mises—"

"Right. But if I tell him I really like him but he's just got too much money, he'll get epileptic."

"Apoplet—" I stopped, realized, and smiled. Amy could always make me laugh. Now, that's power.

"But I don't want him to think he can control me—"

"Don't worry. No one'll control *you*."

"But because of the discrepancy in bank accounts, he'd naturally assume...you know, it'd be his power over me. I need to remain free—"

"I know, it's too bad it has to be that way." I meant it was too bad that money had always equated power. "But it always has and it always will. Just enjoy it, or him, for what it is."

"I will." And I knew she would. "But I'm at the stage where I really need to talk to him about it...make him understand my position, and I can't quite find the right words, the words to make him understand without hurting his feelings, or his vanity."

"*Valorizzare la parole.*"

"Meaning what."

"To imbue words with meaning. Guess it has more to do with the written word, but no matter which way, it's still hard to get it right."

"Yes, especially when 'the trouble' is the thing he thinks I should be most grateful for. I can talk to you. I wish I could talk to him like this."

"You're supposed to be able to talk to me. I'm your sister. If you choose to be with him, you'll talk to him like this...in time. Does he like dogs?"

"Loves dogs."

"Then forget how much money he has. Marry the guy!"

"Speaking of dogs—"

"Yeah."

We stood up and went outside.

"Bogie!"

"Lau-ren." Their tracks indicated that they'd been having a grand old time.

"Lauren?" I called again. "Where are they?"

Then very slowly I turned around.

Amy saw it at the same time as I did. The gate was open.

"Damn. I must have...I'm not used to.... " She turned to me. "I'm sorry."

"It's okay. Come on let's check the road first." My first fear was that Lauren knew nothing about the dangers of cars. Amy got in her car and we each drove in opposite directions along the road which, while never busy, had many blind corners around which motorists would come careening quite fast. As I drove for several miles, I stared in awe at the natural beauty—snow covered everything and muffled all sounds. I stopped the car, rolled down the window and listened. Silence. I called. Nothing. I wanted to hear Bogie's voice. I started the car back up. I wanted to see two tri-color dogs against the white. One more corner I said to myself, expecting to see them trotting along, side by side, noses to the ground in excitement. Then nothing but the trees, branches weighted down with white, and the empty road winding along ahead. Just one more. And I'll see them this time. But more empty expanse of road. One more. Okay, one more. Then I'd gone too long. I turned and drove back.

"Anything?" Amy called.

"No."

"Me either. Let's start up there." She pointed to the woods behind my house, where there was a mountain, or a hill, depending on whether one had grown up in the Rockies or the flat-lands.

"You warm enough?" The temperature was dipping rapidly as the afternoon turned to evening. I knew when daylight vanished completely the air temperature would drop severely.

"Fine." We set out again in opposite directions calling.

"Bogie!"

"Lauren! Come get a cookie! Feeeeeding Frenzy!"

I kept going, the walking difficult, the air cold. Amy's calls got fainter and fainter till I could no longer hear them. I could see my steamy breath as I yelled,

"Feeding Frenzy! Get a cookie! Lau-ren" I had not at first been alarmed, but now.... Now, it was getting dark, the temperature well below freezing. I saw tracks but they were fox tracks. I walked on straining my eyes, calling out "Lau-ren! Bo-gie! Feeeding Frenzy!" Where were they? More tracks, deer tracks. They were everywhere.

Then I saw dog tracks, *their* tracks. Bogie's were slightly larger than Lauren's. Good, then they're together I thought. I started to run, slipping and stumbling. The tracks were haphazard, going one way then the next, round and round in circles. They were on the deer scent. I started running faster and faster, falling in the wet snow, getting back up. I couldn't loose those tracks; they would lead me to my dog. But then I lost them where the snow had melted and the brown leaves lay visible. I backtracked, then I heard Amy's voice calling, "Lauren!" I ran towards it.

"Amy! Amy!" She didn't hear me. I ran on.

"Amy!" I could make out her shape among the trees. "Hey!"

She heard me and hollered back, "I've got Bogie!"

Relief. If Bogie was found, Lauren was near. Fear. If Bogie was found, what had happened to Lauren? Lauren was out there all alone, or—maybe hurt. I walked up closer and saw Bogie, Amy's scarf tied to his collar. He was limping as he followed by her side.

"How'd you find him?"

"He just walked up to me. I turned around and there he was. I'd heard him yorkling." That was Amy's word for the special baying noise Bogie made. "They were scenting the entire time. The scent's fresh and it's good because of the cold and the snow. But I suspect he overdid it. He's limping."

I bent over to sooth Bogie. He was shaking.

"You hear Lauren?"

"No." She didn't look at me.

Lauren had tremendous drive. If allowed, she'd stay out till she dropped. Part of me was glad she was having a life, the life of a hound. But another part of me was operating too. Lauren had problems healthy hounds did not.

I saw Amy was shivering. "Come on, let's go back to the house. I'll go back out and look for Lauren."

"No, we'll keep looking."

"Let's check the house. She may have come home." I wanted to get Amy and Bogie inside, then I'd go back out. I knew if Lauren stayed lost and spent the night in the woods she'd freeze. The temperature would get to single digits tonight. We'd been out for more than two hours. As we walked back, I continued calling, "Lau-ren! Lau-ren! Feeeeding Frenzy!"

I jumped over the backyard fence and saw something. "Lauren!" I shouted. But it was a shadow. My heart sank. We walked in the side door to the warmth of the house. I was tired. I checked the messages. Nothing. We fed Bogie and wrapped him in blankets on the sofa. I went out in the yard to call Lauren. As I slipped out the door I saw her small paw print in the flower urn next to the house, the urn she liked to sleep in during the warm months. My throat got tight. How could she have just been here, playing with Bogie, and now be nowhere to be found? She must be lost. Where *was* she? Why didn't she come when I called her? It was long past her dinner hour.

Please let my dog be okay. Please bring her back to me. I'll do anything you ask. Take what you want from me. Take everything I have, but please let my dog be okay.

At that moment, I prayed to all and any of the Gods who would hear me and maybe take pity on my particular case.

I turned to go back inside, but the vulnerable paw print shouted out to me, "*Lauren, Lauren!*" as I stared down at it. I couldn't stop looking at it. It was her.

"Amy, I'm going back out where we were, where you found Bogie."

"I'll go to the front, the other side of the creek. At one time I thought I heard them there."

"No, you stay inside. You're shaking. Stay with Bogie."

"I will not. He's fine."

I didn't argue, and I set off back up the hill, into the woods behind my house, and into the foreboding dark and cold to follow the tracks again. She was probably long gone. But the tracks were the only thing I had to go by."

"Feeeding Frenzy! Lauren!"

I knew I was losing my voice. I walked, ran, tripped, stumbled, called her name, and thought about her warm soft body, her head, her eyes. "Lau-ren!" I found the tracks again, but they seemed now to mock me. I went farther and farther into the woods, down ravines and back up hills. It was completely dark, except for the white of the snow. It must have been near midnight. "Lauren!" I reached the crest of a hill and stopped, turning completely around. I was scared, but not of the darkness or the woods or the cold. I kept going. I must have walked for two or three miles. This way, then that way, until I saw I was getting nowhere. I turned around, then I realized I was lost.

I would follow my own footprints back. Going forward I had had hope. Turning around I was filled with despair. Now I couldn't even picture her coming up to me in the snow from the distance. I followed my footprints, and then I saw some tracks much larger than my own. I froze. They were walking next to mine. I looked around. Silence. Don't be silly, they must be old tracks. Then the thought struck. What if someone's taken Lauren? For an instant I felt I was going to snap. But the idea was so preposterous...I tried to think like Amy, "Come on Kay, who would steal Lauren? Who'd *want* her?" I pushed the unwelcome thought from my mind. I put the large footprints out as well, willed Lauren to come back to me, and kept walking. I had a good sense of direction, but I was still disoriented from all the similar-looking trees and the white snow. Down the hill to darkness and damp. Up, slowly, no stars tonight.

And then the snow. The snow came lightly at first, falling from the night sky, but with every step I pushed forward it seemed to build up momentum until it was falling heavily, even through the trees, stinging my face. It should have been beautiful. I should have lifted my face to greet it, lain down on my back, but tonight I didn't want the elements, however splendid. Not tonight. Lauren. Oh, my sweet Lauren, where are you? Nothing made sense. I walked on. I thought I heard a car horn. I turned in its direction, stopped, realized I didn't know anymore what I was doing, turned back again. I walked, still calling with what was left of my voice, "Feeeding Frenzy! Come get a cookie, Lau-ren! Lau-ren!" But I didn't have the same hope as before. My clothes were soaked and clung to my shivering body. I couldn't feel my feet.

Then I remembered I'd heard somewhere that positive and negative energy were far more significant than we humans understood them to be. Negative thoughts begot negative happenings. Positive thoughts could bring good fortune. Quickly I pictured her cold and shivering, trotting to me. Me, racing toward her, scooping her up, clasping her to my chest, making her warm and safe. But when I strained my eyes I saw no dog, just the towering trees and swirling snow, and I knew I was doubtful now not hopeful. Then I could make out the lights of my house through the trees and I realized I was almost out of the woods. What now? I would not leave Lauren out here in this alone.

"Beep! beep! beep! beep!" The sound of the horn again. I dared not let my heart leap, but it did anyway ignoring me. "Beep! beep! beep! beep!" I ran up to the house, past it into the front yard and out to the road as Amy drove up yelling, "I found her!"

I slipped going down the bank and crashed into the side of Amy's car.

"Calm down, if you die who will take care of Lauren?"

"Where was—"

"She's not in the car. She's inside with Bogie where it's warm. I didn't know where you were or how to find you."

Without another word, I ran back to the house. I ran in the door not noticing the small paw print this time and into the living room where Amy and I had, hours ago, talked while Bogie and Lauren frolicked, then escaped. There on the sofa she lay. She was covered in blankets, but her tail thumped underneath when she saw me, and her ears turned inside out.

"Lauren." I touched her sides and felt her shivering. She started coughing as Amy walked in.

I looked up at Amy, "Where was she?"

"Right where you'd expect her to be."

"I don't get it."

"I drove that way," she pointed "and looked up your neighbor's driveway, and who should I see waddling down. Then I noticed the knocked-over trash cans behind her. I called her and she turned over on her back. She wouldn't come so I went to her, picked her up. She was shaking really hard. But the cold didn't stop her from looking for food, did it?"

"But I drove up that way."

"They must have been on the scent of the deer at that point. I'm sure they were having a ball. Then when Bogie got tired and came back,

Lauren came back this way too. We should have thought of garbage first."

"Lauren." I stroked her head. "Amy, she's shivering so much. Do you think she'll be okay?"

"I don't know. Keep her under the blankets and try to bring her body temperature back up."

"Okay." I glanced at the clock. "She was out there for nearly six hours. It's coming down really hard now."

"Yeah I know. If I don't leave now I'll never make it home. I've got dogs and horses still to feed."

I stood up. "You gave her to me. Now you've found her. I—-"

"It's okay." She touched my shoulder. "I'll call you tomorrow."

"Call me tonight. I want to know you make it home alright."

"Okay." She picked up Bogie and left.

I dropped two logs on the fire, snapped on the TV, then sat down next to Lauren. She rolled her eyes up at me.

"I missed you too Lauren." I thought of how I'd felt out in the dark. Had I known I would see her again? I think so. I'd believed so, but still I'd been frightened. But she was here. I looked into her eyes and felt her warm body with my hands. Still shivering. I sat there for I don't know how long, stroking her and comforting her, while she trembled beneath the blankets. I looked outside and couldn't see even the Maples in my front yard. White gusts. A cold wind shaking the windows. I watched as the local news said we were in for a blizzard, twelve to eighteen inches. But we were sheltered and cozy inside. Lauren was safe. Exhausted, I closed my eyes for a moment and fell fast asleep.

Lauren's coughing woke me up. She was wheezing and coughing frequently. Her breathing was strained. She sat up and moved her head around to find the position that would let in the most air. I knew all the signs. She tried to gag up fluid, but nothing came out. She kept coughing.

The phone rang. Amy. I told her what was happening, that I was taking Lauren to the emergency vets.

Silence. Then, "You won't be able to drive, Kay. I almost didn't make it home, and it's far worse now."

I peered out my front window to the road, but I couldn't see it.

The snow was piled high and still coming down.

"Well, I've gotta try. I'm going."

"No. Don't." Amy was firm. "Stay where you are, warm. If you go out now and slip off the road... Kay, listen to me. Stay there, it's not long till dawn anyway. The snowplows will be coming around."

I knew she was right. I knew there was absolutely nothing I could do at this point. Terror tugged at my insides. I had no antibiotics in the house. What had I been thinking not to always keep them on hand?

"Kay?"

"Yeah, I hear you. I took her off the Baytril about two weeks ago when she finished the container. I was afraid she was building up a tolerance to it. I have none in the house."

Amy understood the importance of getting the medicine into Lauren's system quickly. Treating the pneumonia early was how we'd been able to fight it successfully each time.

"Keep her warm. Comfort her as best you can."

"If only I had thought to..."

"Don't, Kay."

When I didn't respond, she said, "She's going to make it. Come on, you know that don't you?"

"Yeah."

"Okay. Call me in the morning."

There was nothing anyone could say.

I wanted to act, but I remained in the same spot, as still as the furniture on which I sat. Then I began cheerfully telling Lauren about all the food in all the new restaurants we would eat, but she was so uncomfortable she didn't care.

We were together side by side as we were so often. Just like many nights when she'd lie down beside me, then throw her head back, roll her eyes to stare into mine, muzzle pointing straight up in the air.

But this time was different. She put her head back and looked up at me. Yet, when usually she just stared with her searching brown eyes and was silent, this time puffy little coughs came from her mouth. She shivered. And I shivered. Her look implored me to do something to help her. I stared back at her, and gently pulled her dewlaps and kept telling her weasel jokes—kept telling her it'd be okay.

145

Lauren spoke to my soul. When I looked at her I saw everything in life I loved. She was honor, truth, courage, beauty and love. I've never pretended to understand love. It is either life's greatest gift, or it is a human attempt to create something divine. I reached under the blanket and took a hold of one white foot and held it in my hand.

I looked at my watch a hundred times. Four more hours. I'd leave in the morning even if the snowplow hadn't come. At least it'd be light and I could see the road.

We sat. We sat there, together, like so many other times. Just the two of us. But this was different. And we sat.

"I love you weasel..." I looked deep into her eyes and spoke the next words slowly, "...no matter what."

She coughed. I stroked her head then lay down next to her on the sofa. I held her all night as close to me as I could. Her coughing was intermittent, her shivering violent. Then I nodded off.

When I woke, the sun's rays were breaking and Lauren was still alive.

I heard the noise of the snowplow down the road and tears filled my eyes. I kept her in her blankets as I carried her to the car. I cranked up the heater. Then I drove like hell.

The emergency vet is back behind some buildings, off the main highway. I always had the same feeling dropping Lauren off, and the same feeling picking her up. They were two different feelings. When I'd drive by the turn-off for the emergency vet when Lauren was healthy, my response was relief that I wasn't turning in, but an eerie relief. I guess that building was a now part of my life.

The young technician took Lauren from me, and I watched her walk away, Lauren looking back at me over her shoulder. They would, I knew, quickly hook my dog up to IVs in the back. I wanted to stay with her, but I could not.

When I called that afternoon they told me she wasn't ready to go home, but I could visit her. I drove into town. They handed her to me, with all her tubes in, and she wagged her tail.

"You can take her outside. Go ahead, see if she'll use the bathroom."

I set her on the cold asphalt, and, still weak, she toppled over. I didn't care. I was more than happy to see her. When my time was up, I gave her back to the technician and watched her face as they carried her away. I didn't know if by now she understood or not.

By the next evening they said I could pick her up only because I begged. I had to leave in her IV, but by the following day I could take it out, and undo the catheter. The vets only let me because they all knew me so well. They assured me, however, that it was highly irregular practice.

"She howled all night long," Dr. Douglas said.

"What?"

"Made a racket. Kept us all up."

"Are you sure it was her?"

"Hey, Suzanne, are you sure it was Lauren?" I realized the doctor was being sarcastic. There'd been no other dogs this particular evening except Lauren.

"I've never heard her—I mean, she doesn't bark."

"Must be a fast learner."

I did not attempt a reply.

"Hey, cheer up. I guess she missed you."

As I held her against me, her eyes kept closing.

"Be careful with her. Give her the two Baytril twice a day. Give her the Aminopholine once a day, then we'll switch her to Theopholine. You know the drill. Call us if her temperature goes up. Good luck."

"Thanks. Thanks again."

"She's a survivor. Another dog would be gone by now."

"Yeah, she's tough," I said. "Goodbye."

When we got home I stayed very close to her. I thought about the motto of Paris, *Fluctuat nec mergitur*. She is battered by the waves but does not sink. Lauren would come close to death and then recover, only to fall back sick within weeks and then pull through again. Ted, who had grown to love her, said she was living on borrowed time. I knew my family was concerned about her, if only because they knew what she meant to me.

I built a fire, took the book from the end table, and sat down on the sofa next to my little dog. She lay her head across my thigh and shut her eyes. Relentless, wonderful life.

Chapter 33

When I think back to that Christmas, I think only about Lauren. Events happened, but at the time they failed to stir me. Linda called to say they'd put down the new colt her mother's bay mare had just had. Its back tendons were short and deformed. Linda was crying. I comforted her, because I understood that kind of pain. I should have understood life's insignificance.

I suppose we can never feel another's pain. We can only feel our own because of the other's.

I recall the cold bracing snow; the candles lit and the carols sung; the lights on the tree and the taste of mincemeat pie. But more than these, I remember how Lauren rarely left the sofa, and when I called, "Who wants a cookie?" she would prick her ears and look, but would not come running into the kitchen.

January pushed into February. February dribbled into March.

Time was a blur. It became driving to veterinary hospitals some-times hours away. It was waiting rooms, different, yet all the same. Being unable to read, unable to concentrate, unable to think of anything except for Lauren and pray she would survive the operations. ("Procedures" they were called. Where at first this had sounded cute, it now sounded ominous.) It was the endless patter of well-meaning vets, who didn't know Lauren's history except from faxed sheets of paper, and who tried but ultimately could give me no answers.

I lived on energy and nerves. My body would stay strong through the worst crisis and bad news, and collapse in periods of reprieve. The body knows. If the situation hadn't been so painful, I would have stayed fascinated by the mechanisms of the brain and body. When you think about it, it's all rather mind-boggling. I'm fine one minute sitting out in the sunshine. Then the doctor strides out and up to me and tells me, "Your dog is very sick. She has tumors, esophageal motility problems, old-dog distemper, aspirated pneumonia and low proteins from liver complications—all, for the most part, untreatable." He merely *tells* me, mind you. He doesn't punch me in the gut or strike a blow to my face. But low and behold, within seconds I find my stomach breaking down and my head cracking. I can't eat food. My limbs begin to ache. How do these messages to the brain manifest themselves so saliently, and so instantaneously in the body? It'd be fascinating, if my body weren't the subject of study.

I kept a Lauren Log and wrote down her every change of behavior, what drugs she was taking and how she acted each day. It helped both me and the doctors keep track when it seemed so many organs were failing her. After consulting with two different vets, my vet told me that none of them could figure out how or why she was still alive. How comforting. Yet she kept going, and later on it was Ted who figured it out. Ted said Lauren was living on love.

Her illnesses would keep any medical student sleepless. I tried not to dwell on everything at once or it overwhelmed. I got tired of talking about it, so I joked a lot. My normal line to those who asked was, "About the only part of her that works is her mouth." But then even that became false, for she developed esophageal hypomotility. That meant, she could eat food, thank goodness, but she couldn't drink water, so I had to mix water in with her food. The muscles in her esophagus weren't strong enough to push the liquid water through without her coughing it all back up again, and this led her to aspirate and have pneumonia—what I feared the most. Almost without exception Lauren would aspirate in the middle of the night, 2 or 3 a.m., or on the weekends, which meant her normal vet was closed and we had to drive to the emergency vet, three times more expensive. Her capacity to do this consistently at the most inconvenient times astonished me.

But at least we were putting together some puzzle pieces. Now we knew why she contracted pneumonia more than any other living creature. And I finally understood the reason behind her drinking problem. The Phenobarbital may have been responsible for the relaxing of the muscles in the esophagus, yet I could not take her off these pills for they were essential in controlling her seizures. To make matters worse in the throat department she was also diagnosed with laryngeal paralysis. This was why her bark was always so strange and husky, unlike other beagles, and also why she snored so loudly. Her albumen dropped for unknown reasons and remained perilously low, her total protein around 4.0. We all hoped that she had Addison's disease, for it was treatable. But she tested negative, and again we were not to know. Add to the above melanomas for which she had to have surgery, hypoalbumunenia, chronic encephalopathy with seizures, thyroid imbalance, inflammatory bowel disease, ataxia from all the different medication, distemper and finally she was diagnosed with not one, but two idiopathic diseases on top of the rest. I don't know why I wasn't in the nut house, it was all so frustrating. I'd ask why, why, why to each specific problem and the doctors were unable to answer. I think they just didn't know. Some days they despaired. But the more they despaired, the more they felt protective of Lauren. She was a good patient and a very patient patient. She was always in good spirits and appeared to have amazingly good energy. They loved her all the more for her acceptance. I just wondered how it was possible that so much could go so wrong in one small dog body? I also wondered how one small, sick dog could impart in me so much love and strength.

It got so that there was always a part of her body that was shaved—head, neck, sides and always a shaved spot on the front leg where the IV when in.

I didn't like the quantity of drugs she was taking and consulted several holistic veterinarians, but the problem was always the same. What to do with her during the period when she would be taken off the conventional drugs, before the natural remedies had a chance to have an effect.

The other fear was that she'd become resistant to antibiotics. Baytril was the strongest and widest in spectrum. If she became resistant to it, there was nothing else to try. I read medical journals frequently, studying the new people antibiotics that were continually being invented. I sought a back-up.

One day when she was sleeping upside down on her back, I noticed yellow mucus in one nostril. Common in horses and humans, this is quite unusual in dogs, and, aside from the obvious suggestion of infection, it's often indicative of a brain tumor.

So when she concurrently developed a head bob the vets again examined her brain and found subtle and disturbing changes. When I asked why, they could only guess distemper as a puppy, its provenance indeterminate beyond that.

I knew her G.I. tract was getting worse when she habitually started eating dirt. For this particular problem there was no cure except possibly prednisone, but as this medicine lowered the immune system, there was no way Lauren could risk it with her pneumonia history.

She would come in from outside, snapping her mouth and I'd think she was seizing, till I'd see the red clay around her muzzle, raise her lips and find dirt packed up everywhere like a mud monster. "Lauren, you don't have to eat dirt. I'll feed you." What I was too ignorant then to understand is that perhaps Lauren was eating dirt to rid her system of the toxins from her many medications.

Frequently her digestion became so disturbed that she made exotic gulping noises then ran around the yard snapping off shoots of grass. If the door was closed, she gobbled up the leaves from the house plants like a giraffe until I noticed and let her out. She acted somewhat deranged, so that at first her herbivorous display alarmed me. But as the months went by, I realized it was just part of the catalogue of Lauren's afflictions, maybe the result of so many drugs, and had to be accepted along with the rest. Anyway, she knew how to take care of this particular problem better than I. Human instincts have all but become extinct from disuse. We use our brains and reason instead. Lauren exhibited a shining example of instinct. No doctor told her what to do or why. But she knew.

There was one test, I called it the food test, whereby Lauren had her blood drawn on an empty stomach, and was then made—although "made" is perhaps the wrong word choice—to eat an entire can of dog food, Alpo or something. Then blood was drawn again immediately after she ate the can of junk dog food. This tested the functioning of her liver. Lauren went in six times for this test. Each time the results came back faulty. Her hemoglobin was off or unreadable or something. I didn't understand. But now I think I do. Lauren knew how to sabotage the results of that test. I think she did it so she could keep going back to eat food. She loved that test. The food test.

Once I walked into the living room, glanced at the sofa where she'd been lying, then around at her chair. No dog. I started dashing around the house, room to room. Then I saw her lying on her side in a patch of sunlight. My heart jumped as my eyes traveled to her side. One second, two seconds, three—I exhaled when I saw her side move. "Lauren," I called softly, more to myself than to her and bent down to stroke her sleeping self. She always looked for the little spots of sunshine in the house, and there I would find her.

Another time she was upside down on her back, mouth open, eyes rolled back in her head when I came upon her. This time I thought for sure she was dead. But it was just her Road Kill imitation.

Lauren's file became the thickest one at three veterinarians. They all knew her. Virginia Tech had a Lauren library with all her videotapes. Lauren having seizures. Lauren's esophagus working or, more accurately, not working. Lauren's brain, and so it went. I told her she was a movie-star dog, and that it was a good thing, because "Someone's gotta earn some money to pay the vet bills." Then came the CT scans, CSF taps, EEGs, EKGs, and X-rays, hundreds, I mean hundreds of them. Too bad radiation didn't cure any of her diseases. And when VA Tech bought some new-fangled $80,000 machine, they ceremoniously named it the Pfaltz machine, after Amy and me. That was some indication of the size of my vet bills. Sick thoroughbreds didn't incur bills even half the size of Lauren's. Every time I came back from the doctors, Amy looked at Lauren and blew me a kiss, "Kiss another down payment on a house goodbye."

But Lauren did not give up easily. And neither would I.

Chapter 34

One afternoon when I came home I found a message from Giles on my machine. I'd pretty much written him off as history. I listened twice as his voice told me how much he'd missed me and that he was planning a visit. I picked up the phone and called Amy.

"Sounds too good to be true."

"No. This time I assure you it's true."

"Do I get to meet and approve?"

"Yes. You'll love him."

"How's the other love of your life doing?"

"Lauren?"

"No, Paul Newman."

"She's good."

"And the Israelis and Palestinians pledged eternal peace. Come on, really."

"I mean really. She's on a good spell. She looks and acts great. She just doesn't know how sick she is, and I'm sure not going to tell her."

"She'll outlive us all."

"Ted said that love's what's keeping her alive."

"Please."

"I thought that very moving and, I might add, apt."

"You would."

"How's it going with Mister Millionaire?"

"Multi."

"Mister-Multi, then."

"His name's Walken. It's good. Too good I think."

"Amy, why do you always think something can't last?"

"Nothing lasts. But, hell, I'm having fun, so what's it matter?"

"Love lasts. Nothing of love is ever lost."

"How did I end up with Ms. Mary Poppins as a sister?"

"No, really. They say there is something that never dies if you've cared deeply for someone."

"How nice. How'd we end up on this train?" Amy was always referring to this train or that train, which meant 'train of thought,'and most often, lost trains, as in "I lost my train."

"*Les grandes pensées vient du coeur.* Marquis de Vauvenargues."

"Kay. Don't speak French when you're in the US. Embarrassing."

"Thanks."

"Listen to your older sister for once. Like you should've listened to me that evening you got off on a tangent talking about fabaceous plants, trying to impress those old sows. Did you get the position? Rhetorical, don't answer. Take it from me, it doesn't sound right. Besides, I don't agree with you."

"Why not?" I asked ignoring her lecture. None of us likes to be reminded of how dumb we've been in the past. "Amy, love is behind everything we do. Love and courage. Remember, when we were kids, the young hero John Ridd who sets out to find Lorna Doone even though her clan killed his family?"

"I remember the cookies."

"Love is what motivates us, not money, not power. Love is the answer, or should be."

"Kay, you're sick. No. Sounds like you're in love."

At the other end of the receiver I could only smile in response.

"I gotta go. You know what, Kay? I do love you."

I love you too, sis." I was surprised, Amy never said that to me.

I hung up the phone.

"Who wants a cookie?" I called into the living room.

Lauren came running into the kitchen. Except for being gray, she looked great. The dog amazed me.

Chapter 35

In the morning I jumped out of bed before dawn.

"Get up, Lauren."

She raised her head over her shoulder, looked at me, and flipped over on her back, legs splayed out.

"Come on lazy, get up! Life's good."

Well-being is a wonderful feeling. Once you recognize it you welcome it every time it arrives and mourn its loss upon departure. I had a sense of serenity and of contentment, different from the isolated moments of pure happiness. But then I began to perceive something else, whatever the feeling is when you've lived enough to know it won't last. It can't. Maybe Amy was right.

Mid-morning I went outside and found Lauren asleep, sunlight on her white face. As I approached, she turned her head and neck to look back over her shoulder at me. I saw her tail flap a few feeble times. She gazed up, as if to say, "I love you." It's what she always did and the closest she got to telling me. I knew. I always told her I knew.

"I love you too, Lauren."

I went back in, grabbed her leash and called, "Come on, we're going for a walk."

I took her into the field bordering the creek, and let her run to the end of her long leash, running fast after her. Then I unclipped her and let her loose. She ran, flat-out like when she was doing "the whirlies" but in a straight line.

"That dog doesn't look sick to me!" I yelled after her, but she was too preoccupied to pay me attention.

"Okay show off, come on back!" She came flying back to me, ears flapping in the wind, all out of breath and panting hard.

We went back home and she followed me from room to room, until finally I sat down with her on the sofa to scratch her ears and fluffy ruff. Again she turned her head, gazed up at me, then twisted on her back, white tummy exposed. I rubbed her.

"Okay Lauren, I gotta go work. Come on."

No response.

"Who wants a cookie?"

She merely looked at me. I was stunned. I settled down next to her and continued rubbing, stomach, ears, whatever, until she started to snore. I had surpassed food in her canine hierarchy.

I thought back to the uneaten rawhides in my Paris apartment and realized maybe it had always been so. I'd only just now understood.

Toward the end of the day I sat out to read at the wooden picnic table, which was actually an old apple crate I'd found, and Lauren hopped up on top of it, something she'd never do in a restaurant unless of course I wasn't looking. I guess somehow she knew here it was permitted. She marched around on it but, finding no food, she hopped back down. The Carolina Wren sang to us "Tea Kettle, Tea Kettle, Tea." Once when I heard its song after working hard in the yard, I had somehow gotten into my head it was "Weed Eater, Weed Eater, Weed." Now and forever when the wren sang, it would be "Weed Eater" to me.

I read for a long time in the sunlit peace of late-afternoon. The big orange ball was getting low in the sky over the mountains, and the light stretched out long. I turned to look for Lauren and there she lay in the last rays of sun. Quietly I walked over to her and dropped down.

I lay on my back and looked up at the great branches above, moving with the breeze. I was not supposed to be here. I was supposed to be in Paris reviewing *La Fille de Regiment* or something at the Opéra. But I was here, and I was glad. I turned my face toward Lauren, stretched out beside me in the grass. In one rolling wave an ineffable peacefulness passed over me and I felt on the brink of something.

"You know weasel, the only thing we can be sure of is change, but throughout that change you can be sure of one other thing. I'll always love you." She rolled over on her back just like me and I reached out to touch her tummy. We must've looked a funny pair together like that. She twisted in the cut grass and made the little grunting noises she always did when content. My dog was well. I was happy. I thanked the powers that be.

That evening I carried her up the stairs. I slipped her into the bed, placing her head gently on the pillow and unbuckled her collar setting it on the dresser, my watch inside it. I undressed and got in beside her, kissing her where I always did. Often in the night she pressed her furry body up against my stomach. It was reassuring, for both of us I think.

For a long time I lay still, as two fireflies raced around the room together, leaving crazy electric trails of yellow. They fascinated me and, mesmerized, I kept watching. Then one stopped and only the light from the other remained. I didn't know if one had flown out the open window or just gotten tired of the game. I waited for the two to continue their wild dance, but only the one was visible as if looking for the other. I wondered what life would be like without the other. Then I fell asleep.

Chapter 36

I'd awakened in the night from a dark dream to the sounds of rain and thunder. Normally I loved a storm at night, but this time I felt out-of-sorts as if the low rumbles and sudden cracks were ominous, presaging calamity. I reached out my hand for Lauren. She was right there beside me, unconscious of the storm and my strange disquietude. I pet her, kissed the top of her head, felt better, and tired, went back to sleep. The slightest touch protects us from our thoughts.

The storm passed in the night so that by morning the only trace of it was a cool, delicious breeze. It had cleared out every drop of humidity, allowing me to see each tree on the mountain clearly. The sun beamed down triumphantly.

But I was still fuzzy from sleep. Disturbing dreams had, in the past, always portended something awful. I wondered vaguely what was in store for me. I found out quickly enough.

That afternoon there were two messages awaiting me. Giles had tried to get in touch with me. He'd finally left a message on my answering machine telling me simply that his son had been injured in an accident, and he wouldn't be coming to the States after all. He said he was sorry to let me down, say hello to Lauren. He said not to try to call him for a while.

The second message was a letter on official looking paper from someone in Paris. In French it said that the Comtesse de Fougeroux had died. I sat down on the sofa and thought back to the last time I had been with her. I'd had the privilege of visiting her alone, a privilege I'd never previously enjoyed. Lauren had just gone through a bad bout of pneumonia and the countess had wanted to express her sympathy to me. It was not mushy, but quick and to the point like the countess herself.

When I entered, she asked if I'd brought Lauren and when I shook my head, "No," she looked at me with knowledge in her eyes. Then she led me into the great dinning hall, with its gilt trimmed doors and Louis XV chairs, and over to the table itself, where I'd eaten dinner many times. She led me around to a smaller chair and I recognized it as the one she always pulled up for Lauren, squeezing it in next to mine. Then I stopped. I couldn't talk, for a lump was wedged in my throat. There on the back of the chair was a little gold plate that read simply, "Lauren." The countess didn't wish for me to talk; she didn't want my verbal gratitude. She saw it instead. As I was leaving she said,

"Kay. You never knew how I loved her company. How I brightened when the two of you walked through the doors. Some people, some creatures have the capacity to do that. No nonsense about her, about most animals for that matter. One looks at them and one sees no petti-ness, no vindictiveness, no meanness. As much as I love my friends, there were nights when I wished I could have swooshed them all away with one brush of my hand, and dined with your friend in silence. Her silence was wisdom. But I suspect you know that. Take care my dear girl. And don't worry, she'll go on for many more years."

Now the countess was dead. Of course, I understand now she was saying goodbye to me. She must have known she was sick and dying. She didn't want me to know. That was her way. But how I wish I had brought Lauren to see her. It was Lauren who she had wanted to see. Lauren had that effect on some people; she offered quiet love, and took from them nothing, the odd piece of bread or chicken leg notwithstanding. But I hadn't known. And the countess couldn't tell me.

Sometime later a huge box arrived at my door. It was Lauren's chair. The countess had left it to me in her will.

My life was changing. I tried to accept these changes graciously. I had to. I had no control over them; the only thing I could control was how I reacted to them. So I tried always to react with dignity and a bit of humor. But there was one change I hoped I wouldn't have to face for a long time.

Chapter 37

Bad things happen in threes. When the phone rang at 5:30 the next morning, I knew with a shiver the triptych was complete.

"Hello?"

"Little Autumn's dead."

"I'm on my way." There was no point in asking when or how.

When I got to Amy's, she was huddled up on the sofa with several dogs around her, Bogie on her lap. I looked at my sister. She looked at me.

"I got a call from a guy. Said he watched it happen. Said a red car served and hit her."

Thinking I'd misheard I said, "Served to *hit* her, or avoid her?"

"To hit her. The guy watched it happen."

"I'll kill him."

"Calm down. He's gone. He was probably drunk and that's why he swerved. Besides, your being in jail won't help me much." She tried to smile, but I was furious.

"I'll kill him."

Amy spoke slowly. "Fine. But that won't bring Little Autumn back to me."

I looked down at the floor, ashamed. I'd let my anger override my feelings for Amy. No, I wouldn't kill him. It wouldn't bring Little Autumn back. I've never been much for revenge anyhow. It eats a hole inside of you and turns you ugly and mean. I believe in life, and I don't think that killing in retaliation, or in the sense of capital punishment, teaches respect for life. But I knew too that many people who said they believed this quickly changed their tune when the crime was against their loved one. I wondered suddenly if a man intentionally killed Lauren, what I would do. With a flash, so fast I didn't even realize I was thinking, I raised a gun and it was only with great restraint that I did not pull the trigger. I blinked. Amy was watching me.

"You okay?" She asked.

"Yeah. Where is she?"

"Outside. The guy who brought her was really sweet. He'd already taken off her collar and tags."

"Tell me where to find a shovel and I'll begin."

I dug the hole and Amy came out and placed Little Autumn's body in the earth.

"Wait," I said. I ran in, got some scissors, and cut a bit of hair off her ruff. "Here."

Amy took it in her hand.

When we finished burying her, we sat down outside. I wanted to comfort her, but I didn't know how. I remembered when Amy had lost Ring, her beloved russet saluki, and she told me only much later how tormented she'd been. She kept looking for Ring, expecting her. She expected to see her around each corner she turned in the house. She'd stand folding laundry, her mind numb, when out of the corner of her eye she'd catch sight of something and hurl herself around. A pair of brown boots. She said she could have sworn it was Ring, standing there in the sunshine, waiting for her. It happened to her repeatedly, often with boots or towels, sometimes with other dogs.

There were days when she wanted nothing more than to sit out in the grass, like we were now, and hear the wind in the trees and have Ring and all the others before her, there again, like always, just one more time. To touch her, to look at her. But she could not, except in memory and I think for a while the memory made it harder.

"I found her by the road side, and to the road side she returned to die," Amy said, breaking my thoughts.

I said all the things one does. I said that Little Autumn had a good life. She was loved. I had loved Little Autumn. Amy knew all that; she didn't need to hear it. What she did need was just for me to be there.

I had, of course, thought about death before, though never dwelled on it. But nor had I ever feared it. I understood the keening the Irish do at the wakes of children who should not have died, blown apart by the blast. I understood the awful wails you see coming from the mouths of Palestinian women on TV who have lost husbands or children to car bombs. Catherine Deneuve said that suffering makes you beautiful. I wasn't so sure. I believed I had learned what was important in life. Life is so vast and rich and contains in it everything we need to be happy. It leaves, or should leave, no room for small emotions such as pettiness, malice, vindictiveness, narrow mindedness, dissembling and so on.

After a bit Amy went inside to put away Autumn's food bowl. Her small empty dog bed, with her name embroidered on, sat stoically beside a chair. I knelt down and saw brown hairs on it. But where are *you*?

Amy turned to me. "She was just here last night. She was chasing Zsa out in the yard. I don't understand."

I put my arms around her. "There's nothing to understand."

I asked if she wanted me to stay, but she said she'd be okay. I drove home slowly. I hurt for Little Autumn, but mostly for Amy. The living go on...living.

Chapter 38

I thought I'd seen the worst for a while. But there came a day different from all the rest.

Lauren had been urinating more than usual. Assuming it was a bladder infection, the vet had prescribed Cephalexin. But when the antibiotic didn't alter the situation, and the frequency of urination increased, while only a few drops were actually being released each time, I knew something was wrong.

I arrived at the vet and Lauren tried to tinkle on the floor. The ultrasound showed a full bladder nearly the size of a cantaloupe. It also revealed an obstruction in her urethra at the base of the bladder, making the passage of urine almost impossible. She had to be catheterized and she patiently stood.

Dr. John scraped cells and gave them to cytology for examination under the microscope. Once again I was to wait. When he walked out from behind one of the closed doors to see me and to see Lauren, Doctor John wore a grief-stricken expression across his face that I'd never seen before.

"Kay, I wish I had better news...." His voice faltered. I knew he loved Lauren, for he always made time for her, even when I called without notice. He paused briefly, as if uncertain how to go on. "The diagnosis is transitional cell carcinoma. It's a very aggressive cancer, with a high rate of metastasis. It's also very difficult to treat successfully. The kindest thing might be to...to put her down. I'm sorry, I...with this kind of thing there isn't much hope."

I watched his face as he spoke, the lump growing in my throat. Vague certainty turned to fact as immutable as stone. Lauren's and my days together were numbered.

"I'm sorry. I wish I could...." He continued, but I didn't hear. I was looking at Lauren. She was looking at me.

That night I lay on the floor and cried. In our grief we all feel unique.

But there wasn't time to cry. Lauren couldn't live with a catheter in her forever, with me extracting the urine, her unable to go to the bathroom when she needed. The only hope, Dr. John told me, to shrink the tumor a millimeter or so, was radiation therapy. I said, "Fine let's do it," not realizing what radiation really meant; not realizing Lauren would have to have twenty sessions, or a month of treatment; not realizing she'd be put under anesthesia every day; not realizing the oncologists would also urge me toward chemotherapy; not realizing it couldn't be performed here, I'd have to travel; not realizing the cost would reach nearly $10,000. I had no savings. All the money I had I spent on Lauren. And, most of all, not realizing then that the vets didn't give Lauren six months to live. They said she'd never make it to Christmas. She was diagnosed in late-September.

I talked to my mother and father. As always, they were both wonderful, offering me their love and understanding. They said they'd support me in any decision I made. I talked to Ted, and I talked to Amy for hours. Then I went home, sat down on the sofa to think, the air stuffy with the silent difficulty of decision. I knew only one thing and that was that I did not want Lauren to suffer.

Sometimes I wonder if we're not kinder to our animals. All around us are humans hooked up to machines, or undergoing treatments that steal away dignity and quality of life. If I truly loved this dog, could I put her through all that? With a human you can say, "Okay you're going to feel awful for a while, but it's for your own good." Could I make Lauren understand? Perhaps the time had come to put her to sleep. At least that way I'd be sure to be with her; to hold her head as she slipped away from me forever; to look into her eyes one last time, knowing it was the last; to be the last thing she saw as she went, the person who loved her throughout her life. This way she would go peacefully. Would I not prefer that to perhaps coming home one day to find her alone and dead, or worse, losing her under anesthesia? Anesthesia was risky enough with older dogs, but with Lauren's added complications... No, that I couldn't bear. I made my decision that night.

I couldn't sleep. I didn't want to sleep, then, with Lauren beside me, snoring soundly, I finally slept. I slept hard. I dreamt that Amy and

I were walking in a forest, Lauren beside me. Hemlocks formed a near perfect cathedral ceiling over our heads and the rocks to one side were covered in soft green moss. There must have been a creek nearby. Up ahead the woods opened up and I saw bright sunlight. We walked to the clearing. Poplars lined the perimeter and one giant white oak stood at the far end. Layers of mountains rose up tall in the distance. A dirt deer trail cut right down through the middle.

Lauren barked, her rough, husky bark. Her ears were pricked and I looked in the direction she was staring. "Rwoaf, rwoaf, rwoaf."

"Go get it Lauren! Hunt 'em up!" I unclipped her leash, and she bolted forward then stopped. Nose to the ground she zig-zagged through the grasses.

"Kay." Amy sounded alarmed.

"I want her to have fun. I want her to have a life. I don't want to keep her in a glass bubble just because she's a little sick."

"There are hunters out."

"Okay. Lauren c'mere."

She paid me no attention.

"Lauren!"

She turned around.

"The whirlies!" I shouted, then turned to Amy. "You know, I used to hate silly words like that, but now I realize I no longer do. I wonder when... Hey sis, tell me again how it got called that?"

"The whirlies? That's what the vets dubbed it long ago, after she recovered from starving, and she'd run around like that, in circles, like she was so happy and thankful to be alive."

Excited, Lauren started to run, nose to the ground, working the fields, sporadically, and not very fast. She was scenting. I could tell she was excited. She darted this way, then that way, her tail up feathering back and forth, and she made snuffling sounds like a pig when she sniffed. Then she took off, speaking on the scent. She ran to the edge of the woods, stopped, then raced into the trees. Then she was out again, running the length of the meadow. She was two thirds of the way down and running fast. I was proud of her, but a little nervous. I could still see her, but when I lost sight of her amongst the scruffy bushes, I started to run.

"Lauren!"

"Kay, she turned into the woods."

"Lauren!" I was kicking myself inside. 'Bad idea, Kay. Bad idea.'

Amy ran after me.

"We'll get her. Don't worry," I called to her.

"I know," she called back.

Then we heard the gun shots. We both stopped.

"Damn," I cursed under my breath.

"Kay, we gotta get her out of the woods!"

I started running like I'd never run before.

"There she is!"

I stopped to turn and look to where Amy was pointing.

At that moment I saw Lauren at the edge of the woods, walking slowly, tongue hanging out, walking towards the center of the field. She was about a hundred yards away from me. She didn't look up.

At that moment I saw him emerge, like a ghost, slowly out from behind the great oak tree at the far end of the field. In slow motion I saw him raise the shot-gun to his shoulder. In slow-motion I started to run forward.

"NO!"

Amy grabbed my arm.

"Let me go. *Don't shoot*! It's a dog! Please don't shoot! It's just a dog!"

Then the crack of gun powder.

The blood-curdling yelp reverberated with the shot around the silent meadow.

"NO!"

"LAUREN!"

My legs running beneath me. Slow-motion. Everything in slow-motion.

"LAUREN!"

The small grayish brown and black body lay fifty yards away in the grass. It did not move.

Noise. The gun again. Pain in left leg. Shouts, screaming—Amy, where is she?

"Nooo! Lauren!"

Tearing pain in right thigh. Grass in my face, earth—

"*Kay!*"

Get up—Lauren, Lauren, Lauren—Must get up. Pain, sharp pain.

Stumble.

Again the gun. Grass against my cheek again. Someone screaming. More pain—Must get up—*Lauren. Lauren. Lauren.*

I want my dog. I want my dog.

Get up, get up. Running, stumbling.

"Don't hurt my dog!"

"Aagghhhh! Laur—ren!"

Flying through the air—shooting pain in thigh—Thud, the ground—my legs won't go—I can't move them—I love you, Lauren. I'm coming, Lauren. Don't worry now, Lauren. Move forward—reach out with hands, pull. Clods of earth and grass between my fingers—nearly there.

"Lauren." My hand on her soft body. Relief. Touching her. She's warm. She's lying on her side.

"Oh, Lauren." Kissing her all over her body and head and muzzle. Oh Lauren, Lauren.

Lauren. Silky white tummy, I'm lying on her. They can't hurt her now. I can't get up. I must get up. But I have Lauren. She's safe. It's okay Lauren. I'll never let you go. Look at me Lauren. Please look at me.

Struggle to stand. Slowly, stand.

Silence all around. Very still silence. No Bang-bangs.

There is Amy standing in the wild flowers. Must make it to Amy. Must get Lauren to the vets. Lauren's in my arms. I won't ever let her go. I walk. Slowly. Lauren. Lauren. Lauren. Pain in my leg. Lauren won't look up at me. Her head hangs. Lauren, wake up. Blood covers my hands. I hold her close to me. Oh Lauren. Please look at me Lauren.

Amy running. Her face is red and wet.

"Kay! Oh my God, look at you."

"Help me. We've got to get her to the vets."

"All right. Stay calm."

"We'll have to hurry and I don't feel so good."

"Kay."

"Help me Amy. Help me."

"Kay." Now Amy spoke in an eerie calm way. "Let me see her

other side."

"Lauren. Wake up Lauren." My leg is killing me. I can no longer hold Lauren. But I have to. And I will. Always.

"Who wants a cookie? She's been through a lot, Amy. She's exhausted. We've got to get her to the vets quickly."

"Kay...she's gone."

"No she's not."

"Kay."

"Lauren you've got to hold on."

"Kay!"

"Lauren, don't leave me...not yet please."

Chapter 39

"Lauren don't leave me, not yet please."

I woke myself up blathering, then lay very still trying to figure out where I was.

Somewhere a screen door slammed. I heard my name. I tried to adjust my eyes. A breeze floated in from the open window bringing goose bumps to my bare arms.

"Kay?"

Footsteps on the stairs.

"Kay!"

I swung my legs around out of bed.

"Kay."

"Hey."

Amy looked at me like a mother looks at a sick child. "I thought you might need company. You okay?"

I turned on the bed and saw Lauren. She flipped over in the bed and stretched her front legs out. I bent to touch her, then picked her up in my arms. My sister stood watching me. Tears of joy ran down my face and I could not begin to tell her why.

"Oh Kay, I'm so sorry."

"It's okay. I'm not upset. I'm grateful, that's all."

"Really?"

"Yeah. Amy she's not ready to go. I mean look at her. Does she look sick?"

"Nope."

"I was going to have her euthanized because it'd be easier for me. Pure sorrow, without the stress. I hate stress, I can cope with sorrow. I was afraid of what I think we're about to do."

"How'd you figure all this out?"

"I had the most horrifying, yet life-like, dream and it went on forever."

"Kay, one of the most boring things in life is listening to other people's fascinating dreams."

"You and I were hiking and Lauren was with us, and this hillbilly hunter man shot her because we were trespassing. And Lauren was dead and I couldn't get her back, and then when I woke up and saw her here next to me it was as if I'd been given a second chance. I guess thinking about the cancer and deciding to end her life forever made me dream something that terrible."

Amy looked at me and I kept hearing her words from the dream, "The whirlies, that's what the vets dubbed it long ago. After she recovered from starving, she'd run around like that, in circles, like she was so happy and grateful to be alive."

Was it because of the dream we spoke so much that day of death? Or was it only coincidence, mere coincidence that we see so often as a sign of something because we need to; though more and more I see these coincidences as more than chance, and perhaps the dream really was a prophecy, the Fates pushing it forth to me.

I now believe death to be only a change in consciousness. We all go on in some form or other, but like Thoreau said when asked about life after death, "I take one life at a time."

That day I made a new decision. I knew as long as I had love to give Lauren, she would be okay. I knew when she was ready to go, she would tell me. Amy had said simply to ask Lauren. And so I did.

We were out in the yard. I began talking to her, she looking at me with pricked ears. But before I could finish, she pounced on my soccer ball and began chewing it playfully. And I knew my dog was not ready to leave this earth yet. She just couldn't go to the bathroom. That was no reason to put her down. Lauren deserved a chance. She was telling me, "Come on. Don't give up on me now. We made it this far. We can beat this one too." She ran to the end of the yard, then back to me.

Chapter 40

The Veterinary Referral Center boarded dogs undergoing radiation therapy, but at this point in our lives, I couldn't have left Lauren there alone. Where I went, she went. And where she went, I went.

Dr. St. Vincent met us the first day and examined Lauren. Throughout the treatment, Rachel St. Vincent offered Lauren and me her utmost attention, patience and experience. I listed all Lauren's medications and explained all her various conditions. Then Dr. St. Vincent explained to me the procedure. Lauren would have radiation therapy every day for twenty sessions. For this she would have to be put under anesthesia for about fifteen or twenty minutes. In conjunction with this, Dr. St. Vincent also highly recommended chemotherapy once a week. Would Lauren lose her appetite for food? I could not advocate anything that diminished her desire for food. Would Lauren feel miserable? I'd heard horror stories from people who'd been subjected to chemotherapy. But it was the anesthesia that scared me the most.

"Isn't it a risk with her laryngeal paralysis?" I asked, trying to sound normal.

"Well yes, we'll give her a shot, ten minutes before that will help her heart rate."

"Could I come be with her?"

"No. We can't let you in the radiation room."

"If something were to happen, would you... come get me, so I could be with...."

"We've never lost a dog under anesthesia."

"Do you have a high success rate with this?"

"If all goes well, she could have six months, maybe up to a year."

I didn't at first speak. When I did it came out funny. "Up - to - a - year?"

"Yes. The diagnosis is always guarded with cancer of the bladder or urethra. It's a very difficult cancer to treat effectively."

I found I had nothing to say. Why was I putting Lauren through all this, if she only had "up to a year?" But now it was too late to turn back. Dr. St. Vincent led me into a waiting room with a soft sofa and chair, and within minutes a vet tech, named Kate, gave Lauren her premeds. Then Bob, another technician carried her away, and I wondered if I'd ever again see Lauren alive.

Exhausted, for in the past three or four days I'd slept very little, I lay my head back against the sofa in the small waiting room. I watched dogs come and go, listened to voices and wondered what was happening to my dog. Life and death intermingled. I floated in and out of conscious thought. I discovered that each individual moment was benign, free from disease. Each moment, isolated from memories of the past or fear of the future was joy; no clouds, no shadows. Lauren. Don't think.

After twenty minutes, I anticipated seeing her again. After thirty minutes I started looking around for one of the vet techs. After forty-five minutes, I stood and walked to the front desk. The receptionists were all busy talking to people.

Then an hour had passed. Then an hour and a half... an hour and forty-five minutes....

I sat back against the sofa wondering if Lauren were dying now and if I should bust into the radiation room to say goodbye. Maybe if she saw me, she'd fight to live. She'd probably die because she thought I'd abandoned her, like her first owners. She probably thought I'd left her alone to die because she'd been so much trouble. She probably died wondering where I was and why I didn't help her in her last moments the way I always promised I would. Why wouldn't they let me into the radiation room? Why can we not be with our loved ones when they need it most, to give a reassuring nod, a squeeze of the hand...or paw.

In that instant I knew Lauren had died under anesthesia and they were afraid to come tell me.

In that instant I knew I would give up everything I owned to be able to raise my head and see them bringing her back to me. I would gladly give up the things I value most: the sun as it touches my face in the morning, the air as it imperceptibly blows the Virginia pines. Just to watch her one more time twist and squirm on her back. To one more time hold her in my arms and stroke her velvet head.

"Here she is. She was perfect, but she's still waking up from the anesthesia, so why don't you two wait here for a bit," Kate said and Bob set Lauren gently on the sofa beside me.

"Lauren."

"She was under longer than usual. The first session always takes the longest. Dr. St. Vincent had to map her out."

"Map...?"

"For the radiation. See? She's shaved here, and marked. Don't wash this off."

I looked at Lauren's hip where she'd been shaved in a funny pattern, an X and some lines, a rectangular spot...but the oddest parts were the marks made in black and green ink. She had dashes and dots and lines as if tattooed onto her shaved skin. She looked like a punk rock dog that belonged to the underground stations of London, not to the conservative world of Northern Virginia.

"We'll come back and give her some salami sticks. Make sure she's swallowing. You were a good girl, sweetie." Smiling, Bob reached tenderly to stroke Lauren.

Chapter 41

For a month Lauren and I lived at the Motel 6 in Springfield, Virginia, Monday through Friday. We'd go home on weekends. Lauren accepted her treatment with the understanding and perseverance that had distinguished her throughout all her traumas.

At first she still had to keep the catheter in, and I would empty it regularly with a syringe. After chemo treatments, I'd wear thick rubber gloves. But as the tumor gradually shrank, Lauren could go to the bathroom on her own. We'd accomplished what we'd set out to do.

I got used to arriving at the vets, sitting in the waiting room until Lauren was given her premeds then carried away to radiation. Some days were difficult with a poignancy that hurt for I realized most owners at the Veterinary Referral Center were treating their dogs so that the problems would be resolved—dogs, for instance, with melanomas on their legs and hips that, with radiation, would disappear. I seemed to be the only one who was there with a dog whose cancer was essentially incurable. Lauren looked better than many of the dogs, and yet within the year I could expect her to be gone.

I got used to living in the grungy little hotel, eating out of a cooler, because I couldn't afford to eat out. I got used to walking Lauren up and down the steps and out into the parking lot, with her strange punk dog markings, stares and questions coming from other residents of the hotel. Sometimes we drove to nearby Lake Accotink Park where we'd stroll for hours. Time slowed down. I thought her last day of treatment was something intangible, beyond our grasp, but then at last, it came.

And in the car driving home, I couldn't contain my joy. I cried silently, all the while stroking Lauren beside me and stating, "We made it. We made it. You made it, Lauren."

She lay beside me on the seat wearing a white bandana with new age positive affirmations that the vets had given her after her last treatment.

She also wore a little knotted up white T-shirt with a harness over it to keep her from biting the Fentenal patch on her side. The patch was to help her with pain.

Yes, we'd accomplished what we'd sought, but it was not without a price.

While the chemotherapy didn't seem to disturb Lauren, the radiation did. The worst did not occur until after we'd been home. Dr. St. Vincent had prepared me for what would happen toward the end of and immediately following the radiation. Lauren could experience cystitis or colitis. She would experience desquamation of the skin around the areas that had been irradiated.

"It is very important to protect the area from licking or scratching because the irradiated area has been somewhat modified by the radiation and is now more fragile and vulnerable to even slight trauma," she told me.

Thus Lauren could not lick her open wounds. I couldn't bear to put her in an Elizabethan collar so I stayed by her side and verbally reprimanded her if she bothered the sores. She didn't sleep. I didn't sleep. Her discomfort worsened. She stopped eating. *Lauren* wouldn't eat. She acted crazed. She'd run around fast, like she was happy, but she was not. Her eyes were buggy with the whites showing, her head muscles taut, her ears snapped back and she panted as if in pain. I didn't recognize this face. She kept licking herself so I put a cylindrical collar over her neck and with her T-shirt and harness she looked like a space martian. She looked so miserable, I took the collar off, even though I knew she shouldn't lick, for the licking only prolonged her agony. She cried especially after urination or defecating, and she'd spin around trying to alleviate her burning skin. I hated myself as I wrestled her on the bed to wash out her sores and she hollered and afterwards lay whimpering. In the past she had never cried nor complained. Now she yelped out if I touched her. She even growled at me, something she had never in all her life done. One day, as I was attempting to swab Silver Sulfadiazine cream onto her sores, she snapped her head around to bite me, her canines next to my arm. Then she stopped, mouth still open, and simply stared up at me with pleading eyes. She *could not* bite me. She was in pain, but couldn't bring herself to bite me for she loved me. I stared at her and in her look I saw the toll physical suffering takes on a being. What I had sought so hard to avoid, I had caused.

I believe the greatest torment man can experience is to watch suffering inflicted on his loved ones. He will take torture to his own body before watching it happen to his loved ones, especially when he can do nothing to stop it.

The darkest moment that I have ever known came one evening, sitting on my bed beside Lauren. I had finally realized that I must use the Elizabethan collar. Wearing the collar, Lauren looked up at me with an expression of pure misery, as if to beseech me with, "Why? How could you have done all this to me?" Then she began to flop around, at first dazed, then fanatically, like a fish far from water. I tried to comfort her, but she didn't want to be touched. So I sat there, impotent, unable to relieve even some of her suffering, and I realized I had made an irrevocable error. I had failed the one being I loved most in the world.

But then, like the sun breaking through clouds after a steady rain, Lauren began to heal. Her good spirits came back, and then so too did mine.

She regained her appetite. I fed her multiple vitamin supplements and changed her to a raw food diet, buying the best beef, free from additives, and pureeing fresh vegetables for her weekly.

Slowly our old life came back to us, yet differently; the abiding specter of cancer, not forgotten, but not allowed center stage either. We had to get on with living.

And it was Lauren who taught me to enjoy these moments that would never come back to me. And perhaps the knowledge that her loss was now so inevitable made the having sweeter still. Many the moment when I would stop, and in some Faustian trance, look at her and speak silently to myself:

> "Stay moment stay,
> Thou art so fair."

I knew that I loved this dog in a way that I had never felt before and realized I would never feel again. La Bruyere wrote, "*L'on n'aime bien qu'une fois: c'est la première. Les amours qui suivent sont moins involontaires.* One loves well but one time. The first time. The loves that follow are less involuntary."

Love is a strange thing, beautiful and all encompassing, and I kept refinding it in so many facets, so many approaches. Odd as it may sound, with her beside me, I could do anything. I had no fears. Maybe it's true what they say about everlasting love coming along once in a lifetime. Mine would have to be with a dog.

Chapter 42

Lauren made it to Christmas and then to the New Year. She made it to see the Spring return, and with Spring and its fruit trees and redbud and dogwood, came the promise of hope.

Lauren twisted around on the newly cut grass doing the squirmies, hopped up and down for the Feeding Frenzy, and even resumed bunny hunting, although she never caught one. Slowly it dawned on me how she had made it through. Lauren truly was living on love.

Looking through my wallet one day I found a restaurant stub from the Restaurant L'Epoque, and in my handwriting, "with weasel" and the date. I'd done a lot of thinking over the last year. I decided to give up the apartment in Paris. My parents were stunned, for they knew what it meant to me. "It's too expensive, too small, and too noisy," I joked to them. What I didn't tell them is that I wanted to walk out the door for the last time with Lauren beside me.

And so we left, one last time, for Paris.

The butcher shop was still there, so was the boulangerie. But Roland was gone and Jimmy was gone. *Plus que ça change....* Relentless, predictable life.

On our first morning, we headed down the rue Cardinal Lemoine, across the blvd. St-Germain, past La Tour d'Argent, crossing over the Seine on the pont de l'Archeveche. I stood for a moment on the bridge and lifted Lauren to look at the view of Notre Dame, remembering that first taxi ride into the city with her, so long ago. Then we set foot on the Ile St-Louis, that little ship of an island, its narrow streets sometimes so saturated with tourists—-but then, who can blame them? Everybody loves the Ile St-Louis.

An old lady stopped me on the street and asked if she could touch Lauren. She told me she just lost her thirteen-year-old poodle, her companion in life. And she knows she won't get another dog, because she knows she'll be next to go. She'll be soon joining the little apricot poodle. I picked up Lauren and let the old lady stroke her. I stood there as she told me how the little poodle died in her arms in bed. I was hungry, but I'd stand and listen to her all day. I understood, I truly did. I was sympathetic by way of thinking of my own dog. I tried to focus on the apricot poodle.

WE WALK SLOWLY around encircling the island completely, starting westward on the quai d'Orleans. Some of the leaves from the plane trees are beginning to fall. I walk down the steps to sit at the water's edge for a bit as Lauren walks to the end of her leash and sniffs, then turns around as if to say, "Come on, get up." She always has energy at the start of our walks. I stare at the water, barely rippling. I try to read which direction it flows, but cannot. Yet of course I know, for it's how the right and left banks were named. If you stand on the island facing the direction the river moves, the left bank is to your left and the right is respectively to your right. But it appears today to be stagnant. What history the Seine has silently witnessed. What lurks beneath its somber surface? Suicides. Hidden treasures. People talk of cows and deer. I decide not to meditate upon the polluted underside of the river, and raise my eyes instead to the solidness of buildings and trees.

We walk around going back up to street level and walk east along the quai de Bourbon, passing the mansion where Camille Claudel worked before they took her away. Everywhere I look I see perfectly proportioned seventeenth-century houses, and I can't imagine that this was once the Island of the Cows and nothing but grassland. Past the Hôtel de Lauzun and the manor house on the end that the Rothschilds own. Paris bespeaks her illustrious ancestors. Past the little Square Barye where the boys go to meet each other, and then back along the quai Béthune. I pick Lauren up and sit on a bench looking back towards my neighborhood and the Pantheon towering above. We've walked this island so many times, like so many others before us. I want Lauren's little footprints to become a part of its history, but sitting there in my arms looking back at me, she doesn't care about that.

Now we turn and cut across the island. There's a line in front of

Berthillon, the famous ice cream parlor. The French are very logical; they close the ice cream shop in August, the hottest month. It will remain open all winter, however. We cross the island on the rue des Deux Ponts, and walk over to the right bank and the Marais on the Pont Mairie. I pause for this view too, the formidable Conciergerie.

As I WALKED through Haussmann's Paris I thought it strange how I could have walked these very streets so many years ago, the same streets, the same buildings lining them, yet felt such different sensations from now. Lauren shuffled along beside me, content to be sniffing the scents of other dogs once more. And I couldn't begin to tell anyone what it meant to have her there with me still, there beside me.

I knew where we would eat that first evening. The air was cool, but I requested an outside table and the young waiter reluctantly set one up for me. We sat side by side outside at Le Zephyr in the twentieth *arrondissement*. I ordered my meal, eating quietly, feeding Lauren bites and smiling at the people who walked by and looked at us. As I sat, I remembered, and I felt overcome with gratitude for the life I had lived and for the life that was still ahead.

I always wrote the date on the back of the restaurant tickets where I had eaten with Lauren. Had I looked on the back of the receipt from those many years ago at Le Zephyr, I would have found not only the date and "with Lauren" scribbled down, but also a quotation from Alfred de Musset. It read:

> *Un souvenir heureux est*
> *peut-être sur terre,*
> *Plus vrai que le bonheur.*

I looked over at Lauren there beside me like always. Her face was now all white. She looked up and into my eyes. In all my life, I have never known such sustained happiness as that which I've felt when with her.

When we got home that evening I wanted to talk to somebody. I phoned Amy.

"Hey Amy?"

"What."

"Did you hear about the man with the flink of cows?"

"Shut up, Kay."

"Hey Amy?"

"What."

"You know, the Germans don't really call hippos *fluss pherds*. The term's not really used."

"So what are they called then?"

"*Nil pherd*."

"What?"

"*Nil pherd*. That's the more common usage. Nile horses. I guess there are a lot of hippos in the Nile."

"Dummy, the Nile's in Egypt, not Germany."

"Oh really!"

"So where'd you hear that?"

"From a German, where else?"

"Forget it. I like *fluss pherd* better."

"Yeah, me too."

Chapter 43

Walking back from the fourteenth arrondissement one day, Lauren and I cut through the Luxembourg gardens.

We walked by the espaliered fruit trees and the Statue of Liberty. The flowers were blooming; everything was the same, only I had changed.

I saw Marie de' Medici; I saw Anne de Bretagne and Anne d'Autriche; I saw Sainte Bathilde and Sainte Geneviève; there was Louise de Savoie and Marguerite d'Anjou; David, Calliope, Minerve and Venus; Flaubert, Stendhal and George Sand; they were all there.

I sat down quietly on a dark green slatted bench to think and held Lauren in my arms. Then it struck me. Not only did the statues surround me, but the spirit of them. They were all long gone, yet still here. And at that moment I knew that when Lauren finally did go, I would be okay. For she would never really leave me. I would never lose her. She'll be here inside my heart.

I stroked her head. She was alert and watching something. I turned and saw a lady with a corgi with a brown face and head like Lauren had when she was young. I cannot measure my love for Lauren, it's not quantitative, but I can feel it. I always will. When I think back to everything we've done together, all the many places we've been, I feel that I fill up with joy.

When she goes I'll feel pain, but it will not be painful, if that's not too much of a contradiction, for it will be a measure of my love. Kahlil Gibran said that the deeper a sorrow carves into your being the more room it makes for the joy. And I know what he means, for the joy I feel now will be part of the pain I'll feel then. Everything in life connects.

The more we love the more we risk to lose and therefore stand to fear. But that's okay, for if we don't give our hearts away, they shrivel up. I gave my heart away to a strange little dog and oh, how she'll break it when she dies. But the joy of these days and months and years spent in each other's company strolling, eating, sleeping, learning and just being, will be worth the pain and a thousand times more.

I realize Lauren has taught me more than any creature on earth, for she's taught me how to love. Maybe that's why we're put on this earth, to learn how to love. When Forester wrote, "Only connect," I don't think he was referring to a stray beagle, but we do the best we can. She has become a part of me and, I think too, I've become a part of her.

Epilogue

5:45 a.m.

I rise early as usual. Another lucid morning, the first clouds drifting eastward over the mountain range. The light breeze that is so welcome beside rays of hot sun now makes me shiver just the slightest bit. The smell of gardenia in the front room jolts me to another place for a period of eternity, actually less than a second, and I begin to think that everything reminds us of something else, be it past or present, but mostly past. Childhood—-those early, embedded memories. Proust wrote that the memory has no power of invention, but then went on to beautifully disprove it.

Are memories all that remain after the candle's gone out? Or is there something else? The picture of Lauren, the orange one, stands on my dresser. I don't want her to become just a memory. Memory distorts. Even now my vision of her is in danger of becoming all the many photographs I have taken. Photos destroy or lessen the real memory. On one trip with her, my camera was stolen. Distressed at the time, for she posed quite naturally for me before the beautiful blue-green Mediterranean, it is now the trip I remember the most vividly. My memory, not shaped by the extant photos, is vivid.

What is it in life we remember? The important? The trivial? The horrifying? Always when I complained of memory loss on certain subjects, like the way I'd look up the same word over and over, forgetting its meaning, my mother and father would say that it wasn't important enough to me. "We remember what's important to us; we forget what is not."

There was that tiny, tucked away taverna in Barcelona that Amy had been to and wanted to take me to also. She had the name and the address and I found the street on a map. The place was still there. She had pepper steak and we drank some excellent local wine. But the thing is, I know I couldn't find it again. And I know I'll never go back there again. It's now a memory. Does it matter?

What is it we remember in life? Making love to the sweet strains of Satie; a kiss in the mist under the Albert Bridge; the freshness of spring; the dappled sunlight of an afternoon spent together with family.

I remember the brown face of a dog as she stared into my eyes, with pure joy in the anticipation of food—and how her muzzle snapped, mouthing the words, "Feed me! Come on, hurry it up!"

I remember the grayish-brown face of a dog, lying upside down on her back gazing at me, telling me she loved me with just her lovely brown eyes.

I remember the white face of a dog sleeping peacefully in one small patch of sunlight, crescent eyes shut tightly.

I remember what life was like with a small dog who became my soul mate....

...and it seems like yesterday that we sat under the big willow tree on the longest day of the year and watched the sun sink behind the mountains.

I think of Lauren every day, the painful thoughts lessening with time, the joy of her memory increasing. Yet once in a while I still feel something is missing. Perhaps I'm a sissy. Amy says I'm just sensitive and, needless to say, I like that explanation better.

This time I really look at the picture. It is not good, I've learned, to block out pain. But neither is it good to dwell there. I try to stay with the mood, yet change it to a more constructive, intellectual course. When I cannot make myself laugh, I make myself think. That is the cure. We learn, we believe, we create, but what endures? I give myself a question to ponder.

I take my eyes from the photo and look over to the mountains. They have that eternal quality for which I used to search.

"What in life endures?"

I reach for the phone. I dislike the phone, but I wanted to discuss with Ted something I'd been working through in my mind. I wanted to be a truly good person. I'd decided to give up eating *foie gras* for good.

"Sure you want to set yourself up for failure?" Ted chuckles knowing my extreme penchant for the taste of fat livers.

"I want to be a good person."

"And not gobbling on *foie gras* is your idea of being truly good?"

"Well it's a start."

He laughs, then asks, "You talked to Amy?"

Our sister had moved to Arizona and I felt far away from her.

"No, why?"

"She has a surprise for you."

"Oh great," I laugh. "Male or female?"

"Male."

"Yeah, yeah."

"A miniature dachshund puppy. She says he was abandoned and needs a home."

"Yeah, I bet. Amy thinks everyone needs fifteen dogs orbiting around in order to be happy."

"She was pretty insistent."

"I've no doubt she was."

He laughs, and as I hang up, the phone rings.

"You should get dog."

"Feeling depressed, sis?"

"Shut up. I said you."

"How's Walken?"

"He's great. And you're changing the subject."

"Hey, how many millions does he really have?"

"Enough to pay for dog food."

"Oh boy, then he is rich."

"Kay, I've got just the dog for you—"

"Amy—"

"Don't interrupt. It's a tiny dachshund. His owners threw him out the car window and left him on the road. Imagine how he must *feel*."

I lie back against the sofa lightly laughing, for I can just see her face at that moment. "Amy—"

"You know you always love the underdogs," she coaxes. "He's perfect for you."

"Amy," I pause. "I have a dog. She's with me all the time."

Silence. Then softly, under her breath, she says: "Well, I'll just send you a picture of him."

In the late-afternoon I walk outside. How many afternoons had Lauren slept in a patch of sunlight while I wrote at my desk? How many sunsets did we watch together? The air touches my face. I walk in to put on a sweater, then sit down on the sofa. I glance at the photo. Okay, come on now. Time to think. Time to answer.

What endures?

In some cases love endures. Some lucky couples find love that lasts a lifetime. Love of a higher power; love of nature; love of mother, father, son or daughter. Our love for our animals lasts because it's less complex and more pure. I smile to myself, no, they don't often leave us for someone else.

Memories endure, but as I realized earlier, they're inevitably distorted.

But what else? What truly endures?

I know my own answer.

So I sit down to write.

I love you, Lauren. Some things *are* forever.

Lauren died in my arms on a beautiful morning in May. When she developed a new tumor making urination again impossible, I knew I would put her to sleep. I had promised her that if the cancer returned I would not put her through anymore procedures. During her last week she lived with a catheter so she and I could spend our final days together. And while her body had begun to fail, her spirit never did. She lived twenty-one months from the time she was diagnosed with cancer. Although her physical presence is gone from my life, nothing has ended. As I walk the streets of Paris, a little dog walks forever beside me.

Not every dog is as lucky as Lauren. Please help end suffering to stray cats and dogs. Spay and neuter. Donate to or volunteer with your local shelter. Please help all animals. Boycott factory farming. Buy products not tested on animals.

SOME OF LAUREN'S FAVORITES HAUNTS

Note: The following typical bistros and restaurants were favorites of Lauren's and mine not because they are fancy and serve flawless food, but because they serve either oysters, *confit de canard, boudin, andouillette,* or kidneys.

Aux Bon Crus - 7, rue des Petits-Champs, Paris 1er. Lauren spent hours here one afternoon. The waiter took a Cartier-Bresson-like photo of her reflected in the mirror. For many years, it sat behind the bar.

La Coupole – 102, boulevard du Montparnasse, Paris 14ème. Where Lauren's birthday celebrations took place.

Le Grand Colbert – 2, rue Vivienne, Paris 2ème. A waitress brought Lauren a plate of cubed sirloin steak, despite my protests that "she's on a diet." And before she could pull back the plate, Lauren had devoured the meat.

Restaurant L'Epoque – 81, rue du Cardinal Lemoine, Paris 5ème. Because it was a stone's throw from our apartment, we frequently went here to enjoy the *confit de carnard.*

Restaurant le Vigneron – 18-20, rue du Pot-de-Fer, Paris 5ème. On the little pedestrian street, another favorite because of the southwest specialties.

Chez Pento – 9, rue Cujas, Paris 5ème. Away from the touristy restaurants of the Latin Quarter, Chez Pento became a real find.

L'Ebauchoir – 43-45, rue des Citeaux, Paris 12ème. Perhaps Ted's and my favorite restaurant in Paris. Authentically Parisian, even to the Parisians. No frills, but excellent food and everyone, including waiters, always appears to be having the best time. Don't miss grandmother's rice pudding or, when on the menu, the Soumaintrain cheese. We always sat on the righthand side under the funny mural. Lauren peeved Ted one evening when she kept waving her leg around in the air to signal the waiter to bring more food.

Moissonnier – 28, rue des Fossés-St-Bernard, Paris 5ème. Another favorite of Ted's and mine. The beautiful blonde sitting next to us fell in love with Lauren. Ted fell in love with the blonde.

Le Zephyr – 1, rue du Jourdain, Paris 20ème. I don't know why or how this one became so memorable a spot, it just did. Some things elude explanation.

L'Epi Dupin - 11, rue Dupin, Paris 6ème. The restaurant near the Bon Marché department store where I went with Giles. Great food. Lauren loved it.

Les Bouchons de François Clerc – 12, rue de L'Hôtel-Colbert, Paris 5ème. I dined with friends in the vaulted cellar. Lauren was squashed in between me and a rather large woman, but that didn't deter her from snatching a *frite* off the large woman's plate.

Chez Dumonet (Joséphine) – 117, rue de Cherche-Midi, Paris 6ème. Lauren and I loved this street. The bistro itself has long been both an old standby and a chic spot for those in the know. Also, for those in the know, called Joséphine, not Chez Dumonet.

Bistro d'à Côté – 16, boulevard St-Germain, Paris 5ème. One of Michel Rostang's offshoots. Here Lauren was accused by my friends of being rude and staring at them while dining. She was in one of her catatonic food trances.

Chez René – 14, boulevard St-Germain, Paris 5ème. Just down from the Bistro d'à Coté. Serves excellent charcuterie plates, or what I liked to call piggeries plates.

La Bouteille d'Or – 7-9, quai de Montebello, Paris 5ème. Because of its location across from Notre Dame, this restaurant in the 17th-century building attracts a lot of tourists. Good Corsican cuisine. Many of the tourists took Lauren's picture here. Wonder how many Australian, English, German and Japanese photo albums she's in?

Le Grizzli – 7, rue St-Martin, Paris 4ème. This was the place that I thought back fondly about to describe in the prologue. Benoît, across the street, remains one of the best bistros in Paris.

Les Fontaines – 9, rue Soufflot, Paris 5ème. Laurens always tried to slip into this restaurant on our way home from the Luxembourg Gardens without me noticing. Right.

Bistro Mazarine – 42, rue Mazarine, Paris 6ème. Lauren met a Pekingese named Johnny (Halladay?) here, but of course she paid his flirtations no attention. There was food on the table.

Chez Francis – Place d'Alma, Paris 7ème. We liked to sit under the awning outside and watch the fashionable people come and go.

E Marty – 20, avenue des Gobelins, Paris 5ème. Lauren protested when I wouldn't let her share my French fries. Finally I relented and she got three.

Au Petit Marguery – 9, boulevard du Port-Royal, Paris 13ème. Elegant and delicious. What every upscale bistro should strive for.

L'Ecureuil, d'Oie et Canard – 3, rue Linné, Paris 5ème. Right across from the Jardin des Plantes. A great favorite. We'd walk down the rue Lacépède and indulge in hearty southwestern cooking.

Chez Robert – rue du Pot-de-Fer, Paris 5ème. I loved Chez Robert on the little touristy, pedestrian street. Nothing fancy. They all loved Lauren.

Square Trousseau – 1, rue Antoine Vollon, Paris 12ème. Beautiful, turn-of-the century bistro where the waitress almost we her pants when she saw Lauren gazing into my eyes, then announced it to the assembled diners. Everyone laughed and Lauren, the waitress, and I were the stars of the evening.

Les Zygomates – 7, rue de Capri, Paris 12ème. Off the beaten path. Good food.

Thoumieux – 79, rue St-Dominique, Paris 7éme. It is hard to find inexpensive food in the 7th *arrondissement*, but Thoumieux is cheap, delightful, and serves good, copious meals.

Chez Denise – 5, rue des Prouvaires, Paris 1er. Open 24 hours. Sausages and hams hang from the wall. Usually packed. Also called La Tour de Montlhéry, but, like Joséphine, called Chez Denise by those who frequent it.
Chardenoux – 1, rue Jules Vallès, Paris 11ème. A beautiful, authentic bistro with a big zinc bar and excellent food.

Fontaine de Mars – 129, rue St-Dominique, Paris 7ème. The quintessential bistro. Very good, very traditional. Dine outside in the summer next to the fountain from which it takes its name. What a lovely spot. One of my all-time favorites.

D'Chez Eux – 2, avenue Lowendale, Paris 7éme. Near the Invalides. Good southwest cooking. Huge portions.

La Petite Chaise – 32, rue de Grenelle, Paris 7ème. One of the oldest restaurants in Paris. Lauren broke a plate here. But it wasn't her fault.

Polidor - 41, rue Monsieur-le-Prince, Paris 6éme. Located between us and the Luxembourg Gardens, Polidor is one of those old standbys not to be missed. Everyone loves Polidor and it's easy on the wallet.

Le Balzar – 49, rue des Ecoles, Paris 5ème. Like others in the Flo Group (including, unfortunately, La Coupole in 1989) Le Balzar is now owned by Jean-Paul Bucher and was the subject of much protest by Les Amis du Balzar. However sad the takeover, the restaurant still remains an unpretentious and authentic Latin Quarter brasserie. Great *gigot*. Lauren and I counted ourselves as regulars.

Welper – 14, place de Clichy, Paris 18ème. Ted and I loved to go to the Welper in the seedy red-light district around Clichy almost as much as the Coupole in Montparnasse. Excellent *plateaux fruits de mers*, or oysters on their own. Everything you could want in a brasserie.

Chez Henri – Originally on the rue Princess, now on the rue du Montagne Ste-Geneviève, near us in the 5è. Lovely atmosphere, good bistro fare. Prints of Longchamp and Chantilly adorn the walls.

Batifol – A Parisian chain. We'd duck into one of these when the need to satisfy hunger overtook. Rather good for a chain.

Café de Flore – 172, boulevard St-Germain, Paris 6éme. We preferred this café to its neighbor, Deux Magots for I believe the Flore attracted fewer tourists. I've always loved it.

Café de la Mairie – 8, place St-Sulpice, Paris 6ème. This café must have one of the best locations in all of Paris with the Luxembourg Gardens just up the street, St-Sulpice on the left and a certain French actress and icon in the apartment building to the right.

Café Luxembourg – Luxembourg Gardens, Paris 6éme. I don't know the proper name of this café, but needless to say, it holds a fond spot in my heart, and Lauren and I spent many wonderful hours and afternoons right here in the shade of the chestnut trees.

ABOUT THE AUTHOR

Kay Pfaltz was educated at the University of Virginia and King's College, University of London where she received her Ph.D. in English literature. She lived off and on in Paris for fourteen years, and now lives in Roseland, Virginia with Flash (a miniature dachshund) and Chance (a cheagle: beagle/chihuahua).